DETAILS

A Guide to House Design in Britain

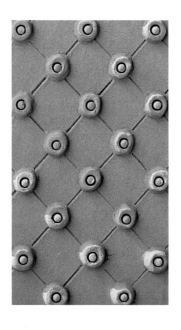

Philippa Lewis

DETAILS

A Guide to House Design in Britain

Prestel

Munich • Berlin • London • New York

In association with **EDIFICE** Photo Library

© for the text by Philippa Lewis
© for design and layout by Prestel Verlag, Munich · Berlin · London · New York 2003
© for illustrations see The Photographers, below

The right of Philippa Lewis to be identified as author of this work has been asserted in accordance with the Copyright, Designs and Patents Act 1988.

Prestel Verlag
Königinstrasse 9, D-80539 Munich
Tel. +49 (89) 38 17 09-0
Fax +49 (89) 38 17 09-35
www.prestel.de

Prestel Publishing Ltd.
4, Bloomsbury Place, London WC1A 2QA
Tel. +44 (020) 7323 5004
Fax +44 (020) 7636 8004

Prestel Publishing
175 Fifth Avenue, Suite 402,
New York, N.Y. 10010
Tel. +1 (212) 995-2720
Fax +1 (212) 995-2733
www.prestel.com

Frontispiece: Top row, left to right: Hand-shaped knocker; Ely, Cambridgeshire; 19C/372/347/445
Bottom row, left to right: 225/Sphinx knocker; Richmond, Surrey; c. 1800/231/Medusa-head knocker; Bloomsbury, London; c. 1800

Library of Congress Control Number: 2003107791

The Deutsche Bibliothek holds a record of this publication in the Deutsche Nationalbibliographie;
detailed bibliographical data can be found under: http://dnb.dde.de

Prestel books are available worldwide. Please contact your nearest bookseller or one of the above addresses for information concerning your local distributor.

Editorial direction: Philippa Hurd
Design, layout, and typesetting: sugarfreedesign, London 020 7243 2100
Origination: Kestrel 01376 533055
Printing and binding: Sellier, Freising

Printed in Germany on acid-free paper.

ISBN 3-7913-2969-3

The Photographers
All photographs are from the Edifice Photo Library (www.edificephoto.com)
and are taken by Gillian Darley and Philippa Lewis except for the following:

Cole, Emily 34, 109, 326, 483, 456, 574
Dunnell, Liz 300, 491
Hart-Davis, Adam 552
Hart-Davis, Adrienne 62
Jackson, Sarah 438, 543
Keate, Andy 240, 428, 516, 585
Mellis, Charlotte 38

Norman, Sally-Ann 150, 217
Pawley, Clare 429
Thistlethwaite, Tom 81, 451
Ryle-Hodges, Eddie 40, 41, 97, 151, 168, 307
Sayer, Kim 11, 156, 503, 579
Worpole, Larraine 25, 176

A Note on Captions

The photographs in this book can be identified by number (1–597). Please refer to the maps at top right on each double page to locate the pictures.

We have tried to date the details in this book as accurately as possible,
however this was not always feasible from the evidence to hand.
We shall be pleased to make any additions or corrections in future editions of the book.

Contents

Introduction   6

Chimneys   20
Roofs   24
Roofing materials   28
Gables and pediments   30
Bargeboards   34
Rainwater heads and drainpipes   36
Windows   38
   Bay and bow windows   42
   Casements and mullions   46
   Sash windows   48
   Classical windows   50
   Dormer and oriel windows 52
   Curious windows   54
Glass   56
Glazing patterns   58
Balconies and verandas   60
Stone   64
Stone carving   66
Stone houses   68
Datestones   70
Doors   72
   Vernacular and early doors 76
   18th-century doors   78
   19th-century doors   80
   20th century doors   82

Fanlights   84
Porches   86
Door furniture   88
Names and numbers   90
Renderings   92
Decorative plasterwork   94
Coade stone   96
Paint   98
Real timber-frame   100
Timber-frame as ornament   102
Ceramics   104
Cladding   106
Brick   108
Brick houses   112
Terracotta   114
Iron   116
Corrugated iron   120
Paths and drives   122
Boundaries   124
Gates   126

Glossary of House Types   128

Index of Counties and Unitary Authorities 144
Index of Architects   144

1 Stone town house; Burford, Oxfordshire; 17C.

2 Stone Priest's House; Muchelney, Somerset; 14C and 15C.

3 Timber-frame Wealden Clergy House; Alfriston, Sussex; 14C.

Introduction

'An Englishman's house is his castle, and ... the ownership of land includes the earth beneath it and the heaven above.' J. J. Stevenson, *House Architecture*, 1880.

Inhabitants of a small, crowded island, the British have over the last 500 years sheltered themselves in an astonishing variety of dwellings. The design of these homes has been influenced by several factors: the British landscape has, in large part, contributed the building materials, which alter in colour and texture from region to region; changing fashions in architecture and ways of living have transformed house shapes and ornamental features; and developments in technology designed to make living ever more comfortable are often reflected in basic housing forms. Through additions, adaptations, reparations, alterations and demolitions, some British houses are frequently not what they first appear to be, but with further investigation many will reveal themselves.

Most early medieval houses were built with the materials closest to hand, which generally meant timber and mud in various configurations. Around the year 1200, builders began to place timbers on solid foundations, rather than straight into the earth, and thus the lifespan of the buildings was dramatically increased. Timber framework followed several tried and tested forms which tended to differ from region to region. The perishable nature of these materials meant that the shelters built by the majority of the medieval population have not survived, although within the core of many houses there probably still remain beams and masonry from early houses, invisible from the outside and now entirely unrecognisable to the original builder.

From these early periods only the stone buildings of the wealthy have survived. They were principally manors and church foundations where groups of people — lords of the manor, their retinues and servants, monks and nuns, vicars and scholars — lived communally, rather in individual houses. Monasteries and abbeys had a duty to provide lodgings for travellers: usually set around a courtyard, these rooms formed a protected communal space which remained standard for almshouses, colleges and sheltered housing. Stone was also used for fortifications, defence and as a means of protection (in cellars and vaults) in the houses of merchants and money-lenders. By the end of the 14th century stone was also being used to build relatively small houses, still, however, for the privileged.

The increased wealth and stability of the Tudor period was reflected in an explosion of building. Towns and cities were growing fast and as a result of land enclosure a greater proportion of the population had inheritable landholdings. More people could build more houses and follow the advice offered by Thomas Fuller in the mid-17th century: 'A house had better be too little for a day

4 Brick town houses; Stoke Newington,
London; 1658.

5 Brick house with pedimented porch;
Abinger Hammer, Surrey; c. 1660.

6 Brick house with stone details;
Southwell, Nottinghamshire; 1700–20.

7 Cottage in planned village; Milton Abbas,
Dorset; 1770s.

than too great for a year. And it is easier borrowing from thy neighbour a brace of chambers for the night, than a bag of money for a twelvemonth'. At this point builders of quite ordinary houses began to add extraneous details to create an impression: structural beams were in-filled with purely ornamental patterns, gables decorated, jetties and beams carved. Chimneys were bricked in decorative patterns, and glittering glazed windows of all shapes and sizes completed the picture.

As good timber was a precious resource needed for ship building and the emerging iron industry, vernacular timber-framed houses gradually fell from favour and brick became the principal building material. Not only was a brick house warmer and more stable than a timber one, but bricks were also much more flexible to use. After the Great Fire of London in 1666, a quantity of new legislation was imposed to regulate the rebuilding of the city. Exteriors had to be brick or stone, and height was determined by the width of the street. Standardisation had begun.

Houses are often described as either vernacular or polite: this separates those built in response to materials readily to hand from those built with knowledge of and an eye to new styles, and this usually means Classicism. The first architectural pattern book which introduced Britain to new designs from the Continent was John Shute's *The First and Chief Groundes of Architecture*, published in 1563. These designs were based on the Classical orders and incorporated elements such as friezes, cornices and grotesques. These motifs had come back into fashion during the Italian Renaissance but had been heavily adapted on their journey northwards through France. Appearing first on the façades of the great Elizabethan country houses such as Longleat House and Hardwick Hall, Classical details were in general slow to be absorbed. However, the Classical influence could be seen in the growing symmetry of house design and the structure of the building. Easier to assimilate were a few stylish motifs: these could be copied from the many books and sheets of engraved architectural ornament that were imported from Germany and the Low Countries (the Netherlands strongly influenced the growing desire for bourgeois comforts). They fused Renaissance elements with Northern Gothic and offered selections of finials, obelisks, heraldic motifs, grotesques heads, strapwork, fruity festoons and triangular pediments which could be carved in wood, stone or even brick, or created in plasterwork to transform old-fashioned timber frames into something more modern.

The Stuart Court too looked to Continental Europe, and specifically to Italy, for the latest taste in art, architecture and literature. Inigo Jones was the main catalyst: he had seen the work of Italian Renaissance architects, in particular Andrea Palladio, at first hand on a journey to Italy in 1613. Jones brought back a copy of Palladio's *Quattro Libri dell'Architettura* and owned drawings by him. While Jones was only working for the most enlightened and wealthy patrons, his vision would, over the next one hundred and fifty years, slowly trickle down to middle- and upper-class Britain, influencing country houses, village houses and town houses for farmers, millers, rectors, manufacturers, naval and army officers, if only in the form of a detail — a door case, window, quoin or string course.

Jones and a few other late 17th- and early 18th-century architects, such as John Webb, Hugh May, Roger Pratt and Lord Burlington, understood how to pull together all the Classical elements in the correct proportions. In place of gables came a straight roof-line and each storey, with its orders, columns, pilasters and string courses, was considered in proportion to the others. The portico and temple front, rusticated basement and ground-floor storeys, balustrading, loggias, pediments, Venetian and Diocletian windows were all new elements which gradually took root as part of the design of British houses. The Civil War and its aftermath delayed the Palladian influence but by the early 18th century it became impossible to build fashionably in any other style.

Classicism was, however, particularly difficult for the average house builder since everyone was aware that rules existed, and there was a palpable fear of making mistakes. Numerous pattern books clearly illustrating examples of the Classical orders (as well as interior details such a chimney pieces) were published to inform the client and guide the builder. In addition many earlier houses were re-fronted in the new style, particularly in towns where the inhabitants, increasingly exposed to passing stagecoach travel, might think it commercially sensible to present as contemporary a façade as possible. Isaac Ware, in his lavish and comprehensive book, *The Complete Body of Architecture*, first published in 1756, gives an indication of the pitfalls: 'The proprietor of the intended edifice will have a right to please his fancy in laying out his money, and it is fit he should be indulged, if he chuses it, even at the expense of propriety, in some lesser article, *though not without being informed of it*' (my italics). Ware was keen to establish a standard 'founded upon what a good taste shall most admire in the antique'. A much thinner book, *The Practical Builder or Workman's General Assistant*, published twenty-two years later by William Pain, demonstrates how the audience had widened, as his book was intended 'to furnish the Ignorant, the Uninstructed, with such a comprehensive system of practice, as may lay the foundation for their improvement....'

Pattern books could also provide guidance for those who wished to build more fancifully in the Chinoiserie, Gothick or Rococo styles. Although these exotics were in general more commonly used for interiors and incidental garden buildings, they do manifest themselves as lodges, gateways and other oddities. Tempting illustrations in books such as John Crunden's *The Joyner*

8 Stone house in town; Beaminster, Dorset; late 18C.

9 Brick house in countryside; Happisburgh, Norfolk; late 18C/early 19C.

10 Stone town houses, terrace; Edinburgh; early 19C.

11 Stucco villa with Gothick details; Sidmouth, Devon; c.1815–20.

and Cabinet-maker's Darling or Pocket Director (1760) and The Carpenter's Companion, containing 32 New and Beautiful Designs for all sorts of Chinese Railings and Gates (1765) demonstrated Chinoiserie and Gothick fretwork patterns used, for example, on glazing bars; or Batty Langley's Ancient Architecture Restored and Improved (1742) which illustrated crockets, pinnacles, quatrefoil openings, castellated parapets and ogee arches, fed enthusiasts of the Gothick style.

The growing sophistication of town life in the 18th century as centres of commerce and manufacturing, with amusements such as concerts, theatres and assemblies, made towns and cities more comfortable and desirable places to live. Land ownership was increasingly consolidated and landowners planned lucrative developments in the form of planned streets and squares which replaced older, ad hoc town patterns. Classically fronted terraces of uniformly designed houses appeared, their elegant exteriors presenting clean lines in a relatively small space. As well as work on large houses the Adam Brothers contributed much to the style of terrace building in both London and Edinburgh, and the name Adam (the work of Robert and James with their brother John) became synonymous with certain changes in architectural style from the middle of the 18th century onwards. The inspiration for these changes came directly from new engravings made from Classical Graeco-Roman work drawn on the spot in, for example, Pompeii and Herculaneum. As before, the earliest, rarest and most expensive publications were eventually supplemented by more workaday versions for builders and craftsmen: for example Stephen Riou's The Grecian Orders of 1768 offered a digestible form of James Stuart and Nicholas Revett's meticulous study, Antiquities of Athens (1762; 2nd vol. 1789). The ornamental motifs that became so fashionable during the second half of the century (anthemions, urns and vases, fluted paterae, honeysuckle, cameos, palmettes, acanthus scrolls, garlands, ram's heads, gryphons and reeding) were therefore not necessarily originally designed for architecture, but came from objects as diverse as Greek vases, Pompeian wall paintings and engraved gems, etc. Applied to features such as exterior ironwork and Coade stone, their style was lighter and airier than Renaissance Classicism: bricks took on paler colours (creams, pale browns, greys and a slightly glossy vitrified blue); windows were larger; the heavy architectural framing of doors and windows disappeared in favour of plainer arched openings with fanlights. These were boom years for speculative terrace building, so much so that a series of Building Acts were introduced to prevent some of the worst excesses of bad practice. These significantly defined how façades should appear: for example the 1774 Act rigidly controlled the amount of wood allowed on an exterior.

The style described as Regency corresponds with the period of George IV's influence as a trendsetter, from the early 1780s, when he was Prince of Wales and George III was intermittently incapable of ruling, up to the end of his reign as king in 1830. The prevailing style was largely Classical, but drew on an increasingly eclectic range of sources for its decorative details. There were Egyptian elements in the form of the odd sphinx, obelisk, or lotus capital, given a boost by Nelson's victory over Napoleon at the Battle of the Nile in 1798; conversely, French Empire style (acceptable after the Peace of 1815) contributed some of the ornamentation beloved of Napoleon's designers: laurel wreaths, eagles, triumphal Classical figures of Fame and Victory, and most popularly Greek Neo-classicism (key patterns, acroteria, thin incised lines, Ionic and Doric columns).

In marked contrast the picturesque ideal created a vision which, in its purest form attempted to evoke wild and untamed nature, and thus create a romantic landscape. This concept, which remained popular well up to the second half of the 19th century, greatly influenced the design of small incidental houses or picturesque village groupings (*cottages ornés*) that could be dropped into the landscape. Although some landowners were undoubtedly aiming to beautify their estates (and house their workers) Charles Middleton in his 1793 pattern book, *Picturesque Views for Cottages, Farm Houses and Country Villas* (one of many on the subject), suggests that potential clients might also be nobility from town who were seeking a temporary retreat: 'Wealthy citizens and persons in official stations, which cannot be far removed from the capital; and ... the smaller kind of provincial edifices, considered either as hunting seats, or habitations of country gentlemen of moderate fortune'.

There was no shortage of designs to choose from. P. F. Robinson's *Village Architecture* even included a workhouse in the guise of an Elizabethan timber-frame mansion. Picturesque details were usually appropriated from the vernacular (at this point often called 'Old English') and exaggerated for effect: fancy thatching, elaborately carved bargeboards, random stonework, irregularly shaped windows, finials, pendants, varied glazing patterns on windows and twisted and patterned chimneys. Rustic work, with rough unsawn timber lending a distinct feel of early 19th-century do-it-yourself, remained a favourite element in this style for many years, even if only in the form of a porch or veranda on a plain cottage. At the same time there was a strand of enthusiasm for what could be loosely termed 'oriental', sometimes waveringly named Hindoo, Turkish, Moorish, Chinese or Saracenic. Similarly, wooden fretwork bargeboards, balconies and window edgings were described as Swiss, Norwegian or Polish. This eclectic range of possibilities remained most popular for incidental garden buildings or a small gardener's cottage.

The speed of construction was increasing and technological advances facilitated the production

of cheap and fashionable ornamentation. Improved and expanded cast ironworks (for example, Wilkinson's 'cupola' blast furnace method of 1794) created not only greater beam strength and an airier, bolder style of building with greater spans than wooden beams would permit, but also enabled a plethora of cheap ironwork features. Improvements in glass manufacture resulted in larger windows and conservatories. By harnessing steam power to woodworking machines Samuel Bentham made fancy mouldings more available. Stuccos, renders and cements that did not fall off meant that uniform walling could be created quickly to cover up cheap building materials. Manufacture provided vastly more choice for the house builder, in an increasingly large market for middle-class housing. Unsurprisingly one of the most influential monthly periodicals, running from 1809 to 1828, was called *The Repository of Arts, Literature, Commerce, Manufacture, Fashions and Politics*. Linked to this expanding market is the first appearance of the estate agent. Early examples in 1822 were Robert Dymond, land surveyor, and Mr. O. Macdonald Jr., from Exeter, who respectfully informed 'the Nobility, Gentry, Land-Surveyors and Builders who have house to let or sell, that ...he is induced to establish an office for that purpose'.

During the late Regency and early Victorian period large-scale terrace developments continued, although greater numbers of crescents and circuses provided more variety, and attempts were often made to widen houses and allow more air into their design. The square, boxy, often semi-detached villa model became highly desirable. Improvements in transport allowed for 'genteel' housing, removed from the town centres. Railways quickly had an impact, as one Victorian (the owner of Basildon Park in Berkshire) wrote: 'We soon shall not want a town house ...all the best physicians will recommend a ride in a steam carriage before dinner as much better than a ride in the park. Cards will read "train off at 6, dinner on table at 7".'

While much building in the country held on to a vaguely picturesque theme there was a more serious and urban alternative in a style developed from the heavy palaces of the Italian Renaissance. Its gravitas was well suited to important civic buildings, gentleman's clubs and libraries and translated easily to housing developments such as Thomas Cubitt's Belgravia in London. Uniform in material (all in stone, or all stuccoed) these houses were heavily rusticated, with large-scale, fat balustrades, sporting guilloche patterns and volutes. There was also a lighter more frivolous version, taking its inspiration not from Florentine palaces, but from Italian rural houses, and often dubbed 'Tuscan' or 'Italianate'. With wide eaves, bracketed cornices, arched windows and the occasional small 'tower' effect, this style of house was eminently suitable for villas on the edge of towns and new residential areas. Domestic, practical, but not too grand, it became ubiquitous. This was the style that Victoria and Albert chose for Osborne, their substantial holiday house on the Isle of Wight, and it is the style that fronts the sea on many seaside terraces built during this period.

Famously, it was Charles Barry and A. W. N. Pugin's Gothic Revival design that was chosen for the new Houses of Parliament in 1836, and which launched the Gothic Revival's popularity. This was a serious style which, by linking medieval Gothic with Christianity, was used to convey all that was worthy and worthwhile. G. G. Scott and William Butterfield, the leading exponents of the style, agonised over the finer points of authentic decoration for the many new churches they were commissioned to build. The thorough observation of genuine Gothic examples also provided models for details such as elaborate ironwork door hinges and foliage for the 'capitals' on the ubiquitous bay windows of Victorian terraces. Their deliberations resulted in an all-purpose Gothic style for additional parish requirements such as parsonages, almshouses, schools and schoolteachers' houses. The asymmetry of the Gothic Revival style on the exterior was usefully reflected on the interior with rooms of varying sizes and shapes; the pointed arch translated easily onto ordinary British housing. There was also a surge of enthusiasm for colour: polychrome effects with banding and patterning of different coloured bricks was prompted by a burgeoning brick industry, and ceramic encaustic tiles, in imitation of medieval flooring, provided front steps and paths which complemented the exterior style. Complex roof silhouettes were a typical feature of Gothic Revival, with gables and steep pitches, dormer windows, turrets and ornamentation such as patterned roof-ridge tiles and cast-iron crocketed pinnacles. Typical examples built during the 1860s included new houses in North Oxford (with its population suitably composed of churchmen and university dons), the model housing built by textile manufacturer Edward Ackroyd at Ackroydon near Halifax, (for the 'Labouring, Industrial or Artisan Classes') or Leeds Model Cottage Society at Armley. The latter was one of the early responses to the irredeemably appalling and overcrowded housing conditions that existed for the working classes, particularly in industrial areas. As a contemporary commented on housing in Bradford: 'You think you have been lodged with the Devil incarnate'. The fight for reasonable housing was a major battle over the next seventy years and many philanthropic organisations built block dwellings, lodging-houses and cottage flats in an attempt to ameliorate the situation.

During the latter half of the 19th century miles and miles of terrace housing continued to be built in and around every town and city, often differentiated from its neighbour only by the name over the door. In 1892 George and Weedon Grossmith's *The Diary of a Nobody* began: 'My dear wife Carrie and I have just been a week in our new house The Laurels, Brickfield Terrace, Holloway — a nice six-roomed residence, not counting the basement…'. But land in cities and town centres

12 Stucco villa; Camden, London; c. 1840.

13 Brick cottage; near Hungerford, Berkshire; 1856.

14 Rendered house; Wells, Somerset; 1889.

was in short supply and life in them was noisy, unhealthy and dirty, so for the middle classes the appeal of a new house in the suburbs was considerable.

Suburbs were a buffer zone between town and country. Essentially residential, the inhabitants depended on the city for their living and never really embraced a rural way of life. Speculative builders created suburban Avenues, Parks, Groves and Drives that snaked their way into the countryside, but were still within easy walking distance of electric trams, underground trains and suburban rail links. The Public Health Acts of 1875 meant that some existing housing stock was condemned, and cheap suburban housing designed for letting was also built. Since it adhered to the minimum standards laid down by the Act, it was referred to as 'by-law housing'. To solve the problem of being further away from employment, railway companies ran special workmen's trains (with early hours and very cheap tickets) to and from these areas.

Taste-makers of the subsequent generation looked for an escape from the worthy Gothic Revival and ponderous Renaissance styles. An influential group led by architects Richard Norman Shaw and William Eden Nesfield worked in what was termed at the time the Queen Anne style. This was the form chosen for a new kind of housing, a suburb, an early example of which is Bedford Park in West London, begun in 1875. Abandoning the terrace, its roads curved and twisted. There were trees along the streets, and the houses were individually designed and basementless. The inhabitants walked through their front gardens and out of their front gate on their journey to the city centre by public transport. Bedford Park was a self-consciously 'artistic' suburb with a community art school and tennis club. The Queen Anne style was also the preferred choice for a number of artists' houses and studios in areas such as Hampstead and Kensington, and could be adapted to the height of mansion flats. Red brick was the prime building material, contrasting with the white-painted wooden windows, small-paned sash and tripartite Venetian windows, door cases with shell-headed canopies, cornices, door cases and wooden balustrading. Ornament appeared in cut and rubbed brickwork, and sunflowers and incidental Japanese-inspired motifs reached epidemic proportions during the 1880s.

The architectural style that had most influence on suburban housing derived from a revolt against the mass-produced aspect of building materials, known as the Arts and Crafts movement. This was apt since twenty years earlier William Morris had moved his family out to the country from where he could commute by train to Morris & Co. in Bloomsbury. Like thousands of tradesman, small businessmen and shopkeepers who came after him, he no longer wanted to live above the shop, and in 1859 he built Red House in Bexleyheath to designs by Philip Webb. This was the first real Arts and Crafts house. It had a medieval feel with small-paned windows, deep red-tiled roofs, rich browny-red brick, large plain wooden doors, generous porches, hand-painted tiles and glass.

Urban Victorian life was one of many restrictions and constrictions and the countryside and vernacular architecture became a growing inspiration for many towards the end of the 19th century. Arts and Crafts architects such as Charles Voysey and Hugh M. Baillie Scott particularly admired tile-hanging, wooden mouldings and cornices, planked doors with latches and strap hinges, weathered oak, oriel windows, leaded casement windows, large generous chimneys and roughcast render — wholly British details that they had seen in Kent and Sussex in particular. They appropriated several of these features for their own buildings, and many of the most popular ones remained part of the standard vocabulary of everyday housing for much of the 20th century.

Houses inspired by Arts and Crafts ideas were a natural fit for new lines in housing such as Lord Lever's village for his workers at Port Sunlight on the Wirral, begun in 1888. Designed by several architects the houses at Port Sunlight displayed a wide variety of ornament, material and decorative features. There was space and air, greenery, trees, schools, halls and eventually an art gallery. At the same time the social reformer Ebenezer Howard was working on his *Garden City Movement*. He planned a careful apportioning of land for houses in relation to land for factories while agriculture, smallholdings, fruit farms and forests surrounded the city with a green belt. Raymond Unwin and R. Barry Parker designed the houses for the first Garden City at Letchworth, where building started in 1904.

The 1890 Housing of the Working Classes Act allowed local councils to compulsorily purchase land for housing. The London County Council built central high-density flats, most famously examples at Millbank and in Shoreditch in 1900, which greatly improved on earlier bleak block dwellings. Further out cottage estates appeared — short terraces of cottages with front and back gardens, bordering green spaces. The more idealistic Hampstead Garden Suburb, which was established in 1906 through the efforts of the indomitable Henrietta Barnett, was a community intended for a range of classes from working to upper middle, and even provided flats for independent working women. All houses, cottages and flats had access to a garden.

During the early years of the 20th century a rather more formal Neo-Georgian style presented an alternative to the Arts and Crafts movement. Edwin Lutyens was a leading exponent, influencing many tidy, four-square houses with an emphasis once again on central doorways, sash windows, cornices and quoins. By now magazines had replaced pattern books as disseminators of style. *The Builder*, first published in 1843, began with detailed line-engravings of current work; *Country Life* in 1895 printed impeccable photographs of houses old and new. These precursors

15 Brick house; Charfield, Gloucestershire; c.1885.

16 Brick and terracotta villa; Hove, Sussex; c.1880–90.

17 Stone house with Art Nouveau cast-iron veranda; Llanbedrog, Gwynedd; c. 1900.

18 Arts and Crafts house; Hampstead Garden Suburb, London; c.1900.

19 Neo-Georgian house; Hampstead Garden Suburb, London; c.1910.

20 Crittall factory village house; Silver End, Essex; 1926.

21 Pebbledash house; Cam, Gloucestershire; 1935.

22 Brick and cladding house; Clacton-on-Sea, Essex; 1960s.

were followed by an increasingly bulging magazine rack of titles: *Homes and Gardens* (1919), *House and Garden* (1920) and *Ideal Home 'A Monthly Magazine for Home-Lovers'* (1920), which regularly published ground plans and drawings 'designed by Ideal Home' with such headings as 'A Very Comfortable House' and 'A Convenient Bungalow'.

When, during the 1918 election, Prime Minister Lloyd George made rash promises of 'homes fit for heroes', the government was forced to assume the extremely problematic obligation of providing working-class housing. Shortages of labour, money and material were acute after the First World War and much was made of the need for the smaller house. *House and Garden* in 1921 stated that 'except those whom new wealth has made arrogant, or on who ancient birth has laid the burden of keeping up an entailed "seat", everyone was destined to live in small houses'. 'The old ample scale' and the 'large house party' were things of the past. A collection of designs published in 1924 by the Architectural Press put it bluntly: 'We have been faced with the old problem, how to make bricks without straw; and eventually have been driven, bitterly against our will, to consider essentials only, and to rule out every kind of trimming'.

For the middle classes, apart from the economy of maintaining and living in a smaller house, it was no longer possible to count on employing servants. This removed the necessity for the complex warren of back rooms, doors and entrances from which servants operated, and greatly simplified house design. Although coach houses and mews had been eliminated from most house designs by the 1870s, a garage for the car was a frequently consideration by the 1920s, and increasingly added to the specification, being built, as the gate lodge before it, to match the house in architectural detail. It was pointed out (by Lawrence Weaver) in 1910 that unlike the stables, which needed to be well apart from the house for reasons of smell, the 'motor-house' could be included under the main roof, and added 'greatly to the scale and importance of the building without any countervailing disadvantages'. Weaver was rather ahead of his time in his suggestion, since integral garages did not really become popular until the mid-20th century. But by the end of the century, house builders had to think in terms of two- or three-car garages, and once again they became separate buildings.

Growth in road traffic resulted in schemes for new roads and by-passes which became obvious sites for new housing, and remained so until the Ribbon Development Act of 1935 was passed to prevent further encroachment into the countryside. For the vast suburban growth of the inter-war years, which had begun in earnest by the mid-1920s, the generality of housing continued to be built in a well-rehearsed combination of the vaguely vernacular (gable, bay or bow window with leaded lights, tile-hanging or half-timbering). Lack of planning controls had allowed temporary

holiday housing to spread in areas of natural beauty producing the reviled 'bungaloid growth' — the 'octopus', as Clough Williams-Ellis called it. Britain's love affair with the rural retreat had suddenly turned sour as more and more cliffs, riversides and hilltops were covered with depressingly uniform Peacehaven-type bungalows called, typically, 'Mon Desire'.

As mortgages became easily available people could buy rather than rent their houses and on purchase they gained the freedom to do with them what they liked (by the 1950s *The Practical Householder*, an early do-it-yourself magazine, had become very popular). A 1936 advertisement for Abbey Road Building Society ran: 'The Slippers on the Hearth — a symbol of perfect domesticity. But there are still many sincere lovers of home whose only disquiet is the knowledge that their home belongs to another. The Building Society movement enables men of modest means to enjoy life not merely as householders but as home-owners'. Hermann Muthesius, commenting in 1904 on the English and their houses, observed: 'The great store that the English still set by owning their home is part of this powerful sense of the English personality. The Englishman sees the whole of life embodied in his house. Here in the heart of his family, self-sufficient and feeling no great urge for sociability, pursuing his own interests in virtual isolation, he finds his happiness and real spiritual comfort'.

By the end of the 1920s the influence of the Modern Movement — the antithesis of mainstream British tradition — was beginning to make an impact. For European architects such as Le Corbusier and the Bauhaus group functionalism was the key, and this was expressed in geometric forms and concrete surfaces, glass and steel. Roofs were flat, and curves were circular or semi-circular. Elements such as copings, cornices and string mouldings were eradicated and ornament was minimal, with just the occasional suggestion of streamlining through parallel vertical banding. Such houses were mainly painted white, a startling look in many British environments: as Lionel Brett wrote in 1947 there was a faction for whom 'a white wall was a red rag, and a flat roof a badge of bolshevism'.

Very few houses were built in the pure Modern Movement style, but a watered-down British version was popular in the early 1930s and generally termed by builders 'moderne'. It was an appropriately unconventional style for flats that were perceived as an uncompromisingly modern type of housing for Britain. Favourite features were 'suntrap' windows, balconies, and flat roofs with a smattering of Art Deco motifs such as chevrons, sunrays and ziggurat shapes. Concrete, though fashionable, was not a material that the average builder found easy to use (it cracked and often became streaky). Thus, until the outbreak of the Second World War, many houses continued to be built in brick, or brick rendered with white-painted cement to give the same effect.

23 Brick house in development; Shepton Mallett, Somerset; 1998.

24 House with flat roof and picture windows; Highgate, London; 1960s.

25 Underground house on coastal headland; Pembrokeshire; 1997.

26 Housing association terrace; Greenwich Millennium Village, London; 2000.

So much housing was bombed during the war that the government set up a Temporary Housing Programme in 1944 with the result that by the following year the first prefabs (pre-fabricated bungalows) were erected on derelict sites, vacant land and parks to house the homeless. Ingeniously compact and set within little gardens they were made principally from steel, timber, concrete and asbestos cement sheet. A later type was made by the aircraft industry in aluminium — a post-war switch from bombers to bungalows. Housing shortages led to 'conversions': in such conditions people lived in railway carriages, shepherds' huts and even double-decker buses. But during the 1950s many permanent homes were created from mews, coach houses, windmills and farm buildings and numerous large houses were split into flats. This was the beginning of an important trend which, by the late 20th century, encompassed warehouses, factories and even office blocks. Pre-fabricated concrete sections were used during the 1950s for some local authority housing, for example at Hartcliffe estate in Bristol for two-storey houses and 'walk-up' flats.

Part of the national post-war plan was the creation of New Towns to be built in the countryside (first Harlow and Stevenage begun in the 1950s, followed by towns such as Peterlee, Cumbernauld and Milton Keynes a decade later) and green belts around cities. In the period of post-war austerity and shortages, the houses, terraces and low-rise flats aimed to be strictly functional with the minimum of extraneous elements. A pared-down functional style created with available materials, particularly in public housing, meant that choices were limited: steel tubing might be used for porch supports or front gates; glass bricks for providing hall light beside front doors; render over brick for an alternative finish. Many of the typical designs of the 1950s and the 1960s involved a theme of panels and framing, colours and texture. In ornament the fashion was for the abstract, rather than anything that derived from past civilisations. The architecture devised for the Festival of Britain popularised a range of geometric shapes — lozenges, hexagons and spheres deriving from scientific models — and these appeared as panel shapes, or in metalwork. Plain windows were surrounded with a frame, and panels of cladding (developed from the technique of pre-fabrication) provided colour and texture using new technological developments in plastics and glass.

Driven by the political need to provide housing quickly, high-density tower blocks were seen as one solution. Quick system building could deliver modern living spaces. As the architect Frederick Gibberd said in 1955, high blocks gave 'more pleasure to more people...a new kind of space, surprise views'. The novelty of height, previously associated only with luxury flats and hotels, was made available to all. Cities in the sky were to replace the miles of outworn, outmoded Victorian terraces that architects and planners were quick to denounce as slums. Functionalism was the keyword and seemingly endless horizontals and verticals dominated the design of over four million public dwellings that were built between 1945 and the end of the 1960s.

Individual housing drew on a variety of influences between the l950s and the 1970s: the American 'ranch style'; exposed surfaces of brick and concrete inspired by Le Corbusier and the Modern Movement; natural finishes, in particular wood, that were central to Scandinavian design of the mid-20th century were also much admired as both calm and uncompromisingly modern. Increasingly ecological considerations influenced more radical cutting-edge house designs, but for most British people their love affair with the brick box seemed destined to last forever. There, in the unending combinations of architectural structure and ornamentation, the British passion for personalising their homes has created a one of the strongest links between the Britain of today and the last 500 years of a small, crowded island's history.

Chimneys

27 Crooked brick chimney; Maldon, Essex; 19C.

28 Chimney stacks and pots on stone terrace housing; Bath; late 18C.

29 Timber-frame farmhouse with brick chimney; High Easter, Essex; 15C/16C.

30 Gate lodge with Elizabethan Revival terracotta chimneys; Highgate, London; c.1850.

31 Chimney pots on Peabody Trust block dwelling; Chelsea, London; 1871.

The history of chimney design is derived from the opposing needs to obtain maximum heat on the one hand, while controlling the fire inside the building on the other.

Early dwellings had a hearth in the centre of the living space (or 'hall') and the smoke found its way out of a hole in the roof. The hole (also known as a 'wind eye' from which the word window derives) had a louver arrangement of timber or pottery which created an up-draught. These medieval arrangements are recorded occasionally in poor rural areas of Britain until the 19th century. With thatch and timber-frame construction, fire was a constant hazard and a thatched house, or one that previously was thatched, would frequently have a very high chimney to keep the sparks away from the roof. Unsurprisingly chimneys were common in towns well before the country.

Once houses were built on two storeys the fireplace — and a chimney — had to stand along the wall. Early Norman examples are stone, but it was the increased use of brick in the 16th century that gave a huge impetus to the building of chimneys which became a prestige feature on houses. During that period although it was easier to build chimneys on end-gable walls, to make maximum use of the chimney (and its warmth) it was better to place them centrally, thus providing back-to-back fireplaces for two main rooms. By the middle of the 16th century sophisticated chimney builders could place four flues in one stack. These were built large and tall and their presence was often accentuated with fancy brickwork or by diagonal placement of the chimney. In Scotland wallhead chimneys were placed at the top of gables, rising from the eaves. If the house was built in the Classical style appropriate ornament was sometimes adopted with shaped cornices or rustication.

As the problem of smoking fires persisted, theories of efficient chimney design abounded. The invention of chimney pots (or tops, as they were first called) was a breakthrough as they increased up-draught. They came into general use in the second half of the 18th century, and as a result the shape of the chimney was reduced to just a plinth for the pots. Increasing expectations of home comfort, plus easier transportation of coal, meant that bedrooms, and even attics, were built with fireplaces, and chimney pots proliferated.

The tall chimney stack with smoke curling from the top remained, however, still an essential part of the picturesque rural vision, and the importance of the chimney as an element of house design was reinstated in the early 19th century, particularly on buildings that might be labelled 'Tudor', 'Elizabethan' or 'Old English'. Tall chimneys also reflected the inglenook fireplace in an enlarged hall that was a central feature of the Arts and Crafts house. In the suburbs the gently smoking chimney, along with the lamp-lit window, became an iconic welcoming beacon for the commuter (a contrast to the thousands of smoking chimneys that choked the city air in Gustave Doré's images of London terraces).

Prominent chimneys featured during the 1950s and 1960s on American-influenced ranch-style houses in the form of large buttress-like structures. By contrast central heating, which was first generally adopted in blocks of flats during the inter-war period, became the norm in post-Second World War housing and the chimney was consequently abandoned. After this brief eclipse the chimney returned as a metal flue, and in retro styles was even sometimes encased in brick.

Chimneys

32 Lodging for clergy; Vicars' Close, Wells, Somerset; mid-14C with later alterations.

33 Brick stacks laid on the diagonal; Godmanchester, Cambridgeshire; 16C.

34 Stone stack; Smithills Hall, Bolton, Lancashire; 16C stack with 19C ceramic pot.

35 Cut brick columns on polygonal stack; Blandford Forum, Dorset; c. 1660.

36 Castellated stone stack on Gothick country house; Stout's Hill, Uley, Gloucestershire; 1743.

37 Vernacular round stone stacks with slate tops on cottage; Grasmere, Cumbria.

38 Vernacular whitewashed stone stack with wind prevention device; Croggan, Isle of Mull, Argyll and Bute.

39 Tudor Revival moulded terracotta pots; Charlton Adam, Somerset; c. 1860.

40 Brick chimneys on terrace housing for mineworkers; Easington, Co. Durham; late 19C.

41 Arts and Crafts brick stacks on model housing; Port Sunlight, Cheshire; c. 1900.

42 Rendered stack; Haddenham, Buckinghamshire; 1960s.

43 Enamelled metal flue in chimney position on terrace; Greenwich Millennium Village, London; 2000.

Roofs

Battlements, or crenellations, the emblem of fortification, state that an Englishman's home is indeed his castle. In the 12th century battlements were only licensed to certain nobles, such was their perceived symbolic power; later, crenellations took on a lesser, decorative or mock-heroic role.

The magnificent timber roof structures of early houses were reflected in a gabled outline and steeply pitched roofs. With the advent of Classicism, it was replaced by a flat four-square line. During the late 16th and early 17th centuries some of the grandest houses had impressively fashionable skylines: pierced strapwork, obelisks and finials. In a Classical façade the emphasis was on the cornice, but options included a cupola, balustrade or pediment. The pitch of the roof gradually diminished from the high-hipped examples of the late 17th century to the shallow forms of the early 19th.

Steeply pitched roofs were perceived as picturesque and were revived in the 19th century, their roofline often further decorated with fancy ridge tiles or weather vanes. Victorian eclecticism also embraced the French Second Empire style, characterised by a mansard roof combined with elaborate ironwork cresting. The later Arts and Crafts style featured deep roofs, sometimes including catslides which came below porch level. Deep roofs were, however, uneconomic and cheaper housing adopted a more minimalist approach.

The turret, originally a medieval look-out point, was an essential feature of Scottish architecture and also frequently reappears in the 19th century, a favourite motif for corner or end-of-terrace houses.

The flat roof was an innovation of the Modern Movement, influenced by Le Corbusier's work for hotter climates where it provided space for open-air activity. The British climate, however, meant that puddles were a more usual sight on flat roofs, and they were always treated with suspicion. Contemporary alternatives of the 1950s and 1960s experimented with monopitch and asymmetrical roofs. More recently the development of flexible roofing material in profile metal has produced a new range of curved roofs.

44 Brick castellated stair tower; Ingatestone Hall, Essex; c. 1540.

45 Turret and crow-stepped gable, rendered in harling; Traquair House, Scottish Borders; 17C.

46 Stone hipped roof; Uley, Gloucestershire; early 18C.

47 Balustrade on stucco terrace; Winchester, Hampshire, c. 1840.

48 Stone with brick gabled façade on semi-detached villa; Cardiff; late 19C.

49 Catslide roof on Arts and Crafts terrace; Letchworth Garden City, Hertfordshire; c.1906.

50 Flat roof on cement-rendered house; Frinton-on-Sea, Essex; 1930s.

51 Monopitch roof on linked housing; Ditcheat, Somerset; 1960s.

52 Curved profile metal roof; Kentish Town, London; 1993.

Roofs

53 Cupola with bell and weathervane on almhouses; Wootton-under-Edge, Gloucestershire; 1727.

54 Carved stone cresting for Elizabeth Shrewsbury; Hardwick Hall, Derbyshire; 1590–1610.

55 Galley-shaped weathervane; Highgate, London; c. 1928.

56 Cast-iron roof cresting on terrace; Crouch End, London; c. 1890.

57 Carved stone finials and decorative chimneys (remaining summerhouse of Campden House); Chipping Campden, Gloucestershire; c. 1613.

| 53 | 54 | 58 | 59 |
| 55 | 56 | 57 | 60 | 61 |

58 Tower with loggia and turrets; Hampstead, London; c. 1870.

59 Clay ridge tiles; Wedmore, Somerset; c. 1840.

60 Pinnacle and polygonal turret on terrace; Hampstead, London; early 20C.

61 Decoratively thatched roof ridge on cottage; New Forest, Hampshire.

Roofing materials

Reed, straw, heather, brushwood and broom were among the materials used for thatching. Banned on London houses in 1212 as a fire risk (a precaution subsequently followed in other places) thatching methods survived by tradition but were gradually replaced by longer-lasting materials. By the Second World War thatching was a near-extinct skill, but the 1970s' craft revival led to a reinvention of decorative effects. From the 14th century stone slates were used for roofing. Generally lighter and smaller, limestone tiles were more flexible for roof structures with steep pitches, while sandstone was used on shallower pitches to create simpler roof shapes. In the pre-industrial period plain rectangular tiles, together with shaped tiles for ridges and valley gutters, were made from local clay. The Victorians contributed fancy scale and scalloped shapes and colours in their desire for all-over ornamentation.

Larger and lighter pantiles were used from the 17th century, particularly in regions exposed to Dutch influence. In the early 18th century local manufacturers revealed regional peculiarities, e.g. glazed black pantiles in Norfolk. So-called Roman tiles were similar to pantiles but with a different profile, and manufactured on large scale in Somerset — instead of the S-curve tubular ridges run from top to bottom; variations include double or triple Romans (two or three ridges). Brightly coloured green- or blue-glazed pantiles were fashionably different in the 1920s and 1930s. Concrete versions of most kinds of tile were manufactured in the 20th century.

Slate is a natural, light roofing material light, easily split and impervious to frost. The Welsh slate industry was developed by Lord Penrhyn in the 1760s. Initially slate was often used where it was less visible but by the middle of the 19th century it had become the standard roofing material.

Shortages of money and materials after the First World War led to experimentation with cheap roofing materials such as asbestos tiles (which were criticised for their pink colour), corrugated iron (too hot and noisy) and tarred felt. Popular for bungalows and holiday houses, some districts nevertheless forbade the use of such alien materials.

		64	65	66
62				
		67	68	
63				
		69	70	

62 Barley-straw thatch weighted with stones on croft; Outer Hebrides; Western Isles.

63 Thatch on timber-frame cottage; Hatfield Broad Oak, Essex.

64 Stone slates; Stanley Pontlarge, Gloucestershire; 14C and later (house).

65 Tile roof on brick farmhouse; Appledore, Kent; 17C.

66 Scallop-shaped slate tiles on Chatsworth estate cottage; Edensor, Derbyshire; 1830s.

67 Slate roof; model terrace housing for miners; New Bolsover, Derbyshire; 1888–93.

68 Black-glazed pantiles with flint and brick; Beccles, Norfolk; 17C.

69 Triple roman clay tiles on stone cottage; Ditcheat, Somerset.

70 Mansard roof with green-glazed pantiles on brick house; Welwyn Garden City, Hertfordshire; late 1920s–early 1930s.

Gables and pediments

71 Crow-stepped gable, fisherman's cottage; Crail, Fife; 17C/18C.

72 Classical Revival pediment; Mickley, Yorkshire; 1982.

73 Dutch gable on early 17C brick house; Great Saling Hall, Essex; gable dated 1699.

74 Revived Dutch/Flemish-style gable on brick house; Kensington, London; 1880s.

Any house with a pitched roof will have a gable at either end, but the gable only becomes a significant feature when it appears on the front elevation. On early timber-frame houses the basic structure was often enlarged by the addition of a cross-wing or end-wings. This was partly in response to the growing practice of having bedrooms on the upper floors, as a gable added both height and light to the attic floor. For the home-owner in the Tudor period more gables meant a more prestigious house, and the addition of a porch often created another gable. Jettied gables looked impressive, towering outwards, sometimes three or four storeys high, but these were forbidden in towns in the 17th century because of the fire risk. Houses in stone, typically manor houses and town houses, followed the same gabled pattern but they tended to be more symmetrical. The space within the triangle was the perfect field for a datestone, heraldic embellishment or sundial.

An alternative to the plain gable emerged around 1570 on the grandest houses, whose owners had access to knowledge of the latest architectural designs from Northern Europe. These Flemish or Dutch gables (brick built like the continental originals) curled and curved, included volutes and small pediments, and were the location for a rich selection of decorative motifs. Sometimes they were stepped ('crow-stepped', 'corbie-stepped'), a version which remained particularly popular in Scotland.

The pediment, supported by columns, is a feature derived from ancient Classical architecture, particularly temple fronts. The architect Palladio adapted it for the façade of villas and thus it was translated onto the fronts of British houses in the mid-17th century. The complete temple front only appears on the grandest houses, but the pediment alone or with pilasters makes frequently appearances on the façades of quite modest houses throughout the 18th century. Unlike a gable the pediment was always placed centrally and bore no relation to the structure of the house. But like the gable it conveyed grandeur and importance. In addition the pediment was used on terraces to unify the block and to give the impression that the separate houses were one grand whole. Few Neo-Georgian houses of the 20th century have resisted the lure of the pediment, even if only reproduced in miniature over the door.

When the Victorians became bored with Classical symmetry, they quickly revived the gable and expressed it in typically eclectic style as Tudor, Elizabethan or Jacobean. When deep red bricks became fashionable again from the 1870s to 1890s the elaborate Flemish gable was quickly revived. An urban favourite, it was easily attached to high mansion blocks and lofty town houses that filled narrow city plots. With moulded terracotta the options for ornamenting the gable were almost unlimited. For garden cities, garden suburbs and country houses of the early 20th century

a tile-hung vernacular style or decorative half-timbering, was deemed more suitable. Partnered with the bay window the gable became the dominant 'value-added' feature of suburban inter-war housing.

A brief vogue for Cape Dutch style from Southern Africa during the early 20th century bought the large curly gable back into fashion, imitating the architecture which the early Dutch settlers had exported from Northern Europe when they colonised Africa in the 17th century.

Gables and pediments

75 Gable on stone manor house; Trerice, Cornwall; c. 1570.

76 Gables on stone and brick double cottage; Manthorpe, Lincolnshire; mid-19C.

77 Jettied gables on timber-frame houses; Bristol; 17C.

78 Tudor Revival gables on brick semi-detached villa; Hackney, London; 1839.

79 Timber-frame gables; Writtle, Essex; 15C/16C.

80 Cape Dutch-style gable, roughcast and tile; Chelmsford, Essex; c. 1910–20.

	76			82	
75		77	81		83
	78				
79		80		84	85

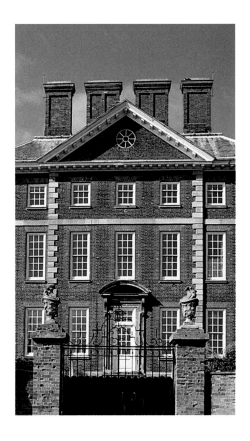

81 Pediment on Colston Almshouses; Bristol; 1691.

82 Pediment on gate lodge to Langleys;
Great Waltham, Essex; c. 1725.

83 Pediment; Winslow Hall, Buckinghamshire; 1700–4.

84 Pediment on terrace; New Town,
Edinburgh; c. 1817.

85 Stucco pediment on Regency villa; Cheltenham,
Gloucestershire; c.1820.

Bargeboards

Also sometimes referred to as vergeboards, bargeboards are wooden planks fixed to gable and eave with the original purpose of providing protection against the weather. Original bargeboards appeared only on timber-frame houses (never stone) and examples with cusped and scalloped decorative edging are extant from the mid-14th century. A prime area for decorative carving, bargeboards became increasingly elaborate particularly by the late 16th century when jetties and multiple gables were the focus of architectural style. Gothic motifs, such as quatrefoils and trefoils, were pierced through the boards and elaborate finials and pendants were added at the apex and eave.

Bargeboards re-emerged as part of the picturesque, 'Old English', Tudor, Elizabethan and Gothic Revivals. No longer part of a timber-frame structure bargeboards also appeared on stone, brick and rendered houses, and the shadow cast by the patterned board on the wall became an important decorative element. Since they are wood and liable to deteriorate bargeboards were often replaced, and some later Victorian replacements were very wide and elaborately carved. They were also added to plain houses to give them an instant picturesque appeal.

Simpler, thinner (and thus more economic) bargeboards feature on Edwardian terraces and suburban houses, frequently in conjunction with mock half-timbering.

86 Timber-frame cottage with original cusped bargeboard; Steventon, Oxfordshire; 14C.

87 Running scroll pattern; Long Melford, Suffolk; 17C.

88 Scrolling vine pattern; Halstead, Essex; later addition to 17C pub.

89 Acorns and oak leaves; Kingsbridge, Devon; c. 1840.

90 Tudor Revival trefoils and cusping; Chester, Cheshire; mid-19C.

91 Trefoils and cusping on gate lodge; Greenwich, London; mid-19C.

92 Zig-zag pattern on estate cottages; Badminton, Gloucestershire; 1860.

93 Quatrefoils, finial and pendant on Holly Village estate cottage; Highgate, London; 1865.

94 Festoon pattern on terrace; Bridgewater, Somerset; c. 1880.

Rainwater heads and drainpipes

It is recorded that lead downpipes were ordered for the White Tower of the Tower of London in 1240 to prevent rainwater spoiling the whitewashed walls. The usual medieval solution — frequently seen on church architecture and presumably adapted for domestic use — was a gargoyle that projected the water away from the wall. Square-section lead downpipes usually with box-shaped heads at roof level subsequently became a decorative feature of substantial Elizabethan and Jacobean houses. Since lead was easily cast, it often proved irresistible to include some ornament either placed on the rainwater head or the horizontal fixing points: usually dates, monograms, crests and heraldic motifs. These presumably often matched lead cisterns which collected water at ground level.

After the Great Fire downpipes were required in London according to new regulations instituted in 1667. In 1763 an Act of Parliament demanded that downpipes be included on new housing which by this time could be manufactured in cast iron, and rainwater heads became a more efficient cup-shape. On houses built in the Italianate style with markedly projecting eaves the gutter became integral to the cornice and was often supported on double brackets. The sight of rainwater heads and downpipes was eliminated as far as possible on Classical façades, and they were certainly not considered an opportunity for ornament.

In the 19th century roof silhouettes reverted to steeper and more complicated profiles and there was a corresponding need for well-articulated systems of gutters and downpipes. These were sometimes appropriately decorated with Gothic motifs such as castellated rainwater heads and Tudor roses. The Victorian enthusiasm for seeking out appropriate ornament produced rainwater heads embossed with watery motifs such as bulrushes, dolphins and boats. Plastic guttering in the 20th century appears to have made little stylistic contribution to this detail.

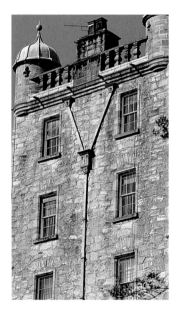

| 95 | 96 | 99 | 100 | 101 |
| 97 | 98 | 102 | 103 | 104 |

95 Lead downpipe and fixing, cast with heraldic scallop shell and initials; Stanway House, Chipping Campden, Gloucestershire; 16C.

96 Painted lead downpipe and fixing, cast with heraldic crest; Burton Agnes Hall, Yorkshire; early 17C.

97 Downpipe system; Drumlanrig Castle, Dumfries and Galloway; 1680–90.

98 Lead rainwater head and downpipe; Canons Ashby, Northamptonshire; 1706.

99 Painted lead rainwater head; Uley, Gloucestershire; 1743.

100 Painted cast-iron rainwater head and downpipe: Great Easton, Essex; 1848.

101 Painted cast-iron gutter, rainwater head and downpipe on terrace; Morningside, Edinburgh; 1878.

102 Lead downpipe fixing, cast with Arts and Crafts plant motif; Lythe, North Yorkshire; 1890s.

103 Painted cast-iron rainwater head with fish motif; Port Sunlight, Cheshire; c. 1900.

104 Painted cast-iron rainwater head in form of Art Deco urn; Castle Cary, Somerset; 1930s.

Windows

105 Stone-mullioned windows with leaded lights; Levens Hall, Kendal, Cumbria; late 16C/early 17C.

106 Upper storey with blind and real sash windows; Woburn, Bedfordshire; mid-18C.

107 Long casement windows with coloured glass margin on stucco terrace; Brighton, Sussex; c.1835.

Most early window openings, such as they were, had wooden shutters on the inside, and translucency was achieved using materials such as reed lattices, linen cloth or horn. Designs and techniques for early medieval domestic windows were influenced by ecclesiastical building where virtually all the precious early glass had been used (small lancets and larger arched windows behind the lord of the manor's dais for the great hall were little different in shape from church windows). Glass windows are documented at Henry III's palaces at Windsor and Woodstock in the 13th century: the king issued a writ that his glass casements should be divided in two down the centre so that they could be opened 'at pleasure'.

Flat glass, both clear and coloured was, until the Tudor period, a luxury imported from France, Flanders and parts of Germany. It was considered so valuable that it was not until 1599 that windows were considered a permanent fixture. By the 1570s glass was being manufactured in Britain; notably in Surrey and Sussex where there was silica sand and plenty of wood for firing furnaces. As with other manufacturing processes the national shortage of wood led to a ban in 1615 on its use in glass-making. At this point manufacture moved to coal-producing areas such as Newcastle and the West Midlands. To make windows during this period the glass had to be cut into diamonds and rectangles small and light enough to be supported by lead bars (known as cames).

By the end of the 16th century, glass was easily available and could be afforded by most although it remained a rare commodity for the poor as late as the 18th century. Undoubtedly seen as an exciting new material, glass glittered on façades in a profusion of differently sized and shaped windows. When set within the lead compartments the window was rarely completely flat, so that the glass caught the light at different angles, creating a rich and desirable sparkle which was highlighted by bay, oriel and bow windows.

Tudor leaded lights were principally composed of diamond shapes, although decorative Gothic shapes and coloured glass were also included and set within an iron frame. These were hung on pivot hinges as a casement window, or on stone or timber mullions. By the mid 17th century leaded glazing was generally in squares and the most frequently used window type on stone houses was horizontal with moulded mullions.

This profusion of window shapes and sizes was typical of the Tudor style, while Classicism required that windows be both symmetrical and vertical (reflecting higher ceilings). Fashion and convenience went hand-in-hand: brick was now the popular building material and made vertical opening far easier and logical than it had ever been using stone or wooden lintels. Thus the mullion and transom or cross window emerged: a cross-piece cut across the mullion dividing the window at the uppermost third of its height.

The invention of the sash window around 1670 was one of the most radical changes to be made to the exterior of the British house. As Celia Fiennes frequently noted on her travels around Britain at the end of the 17th century sashes rapidly replaced earlier windows on existing houses. The sash window was a perfect match for the requirements of Classical architecture. Window voids could be filled evenly with modular square and rectangular panes without distracting attention from the architectural features. During the first half of the 18th century Classical influences contributed to the design of window surrounds: grotesque or prominent keystones with quoins, emphasised rustication, volutes at the base and lugs at the top were baroque; while triangular or segmental pediments or a cornice projecting over windows were essentially taken from Palladio. Venetian and Diocletian windows are also introduced in this period.

Building regulations affected windows in several ways. A window tax was levied in 1695 on houses which may have resulted in the creation of bi-partite windows (since two windows as close as 12 inches counted as one); and some 'blind' windows. However, many of these bricked-in window spaces might equally have been there for reasons of symmetry or interior alteration. The tax was extended from 1798 to 1825 during which time it affected houses with only six windows, which meant that builders made each window as large as possible to let in the maximum light. Fire protection measures in the London Building Act of 1709 required that the wooden surround of a sash window not be flush with the outside of the wall, but recessed by four inches. This had the effect of making the window frames appear much less dominant. A similar act in 1774 then demanded that the frame should be recessed into the wall, so that only a slim frame of wood was visible.

By the last quarter of the 18th century framing or emphasising windows with contrasting coloured brick or stone architraves ceased to be fashionable. The proportion of window to façade had grown larger, facilitated by improved glass manufacture, and many first-floor sash windows reached almost to floor level.

Regency architecture encouraged an easy flow between house and garden, and floor-length sash windows appeared at ground level. Even easier access was provided by the introduction of French windows, described by Humphrey Repton in 1816 as a modern improvement 'borrowed from the French of folding glass doors opening into a garden; by which effect a room is like that of a tent or marquee, and in summer, delightful' (*Fragments in the Theory and Practice of Landscape Gardening*). Bow windows, verandas and balconies further enhanced the light and airy feel.

This was a period of experimentation with glazing patterns. Square windows tended to have four-over-four panels, arched windows had Gothic tracery or loops and circles; both had variations with an extra glazing bar at the margin of the window, sometimes filled with coloured glass. Fancy glazing was an important element in the picturesque: James Malton in his writing on cottages in 1798 listed 'oblong square, lozenges, mixed hexagons, or hexagons and lozenges mixed' as possible leaded lights but warned that they were 'subject to destruction from high winds, unless well stiffened by small iron bars'. The introduction of cast-iron windows (using techniques acquired from glasshouses and industrial buildings) meant that picturesque glazing could be achieved economically on lodges, cottages and almshouses.

By the middle of the 19th century the fall in the price of glass, coupled with improved manufacturing processes, made it robust enough to use in large panes on both sash windows and new large-pane casements. In the second half of the century the smooth flat façade was out of fashion and was replaced by the interrupted line of the canted bay window. Small nods to the Gothic Revival were made on thousands of terrace houses: one of the most common effects was to convert the mullions of the bay into colonettes capped with Gothic-inspired leaves and flowers. A plain expanse of glass seemed to trigger a need for a return to the ornamental window frame and Victorian bay windows were decorated with all manner of carved stone dressings, chamfering, incised lines, tilework and polychrome brick. The 'stilt head' window was also popular.

By the 1880s the architect or builder almost certainly included a variety of window shapes, sizes and types, whatever style he was using. For example the popular Queen Anne Revival style reverted, as in the early 18th-century original, to a preference for verticality and segmental heads (shallow-arched, swept head), and to sash windows filled with many small panes. However sash windows were not *de rigueur*, and dormer windows and oriels with casements were back in favour. This multiplicity of window designs reflected the variety of rooms within: halls, cloakrooms, studies, studios, dining rooms, sitting rooms, etc., all of which had different lighting requirements. Windows no longer clearly indicated each storey of a house, since much was made of stairwell windows and double-height halls. Towards the end of the 19th century window design tended to divide horizontally into one-third/two-thirds, with the top third glazed in a more decorative manner and opening independently, whatever the window type.

In stark contrast to this rich assembly of window types destined for the house, mansion block, or terraces built for the middle and upper classes, the slum-dweller's cellar window admitted virtually no natural light. Housing reformers soon realised that sunlight and ventilation were crucial to the improvement of health and Victorian model housing is notable for its plain, unadorned but large windows.

House builders who were following the Arts and Crafts route returned to the horizontal casement window of vernacular tradition. French windows leading into the garden became extremely popular as the garden became an extension of the house — somewhere to eat, sit, play games in (croquet or

108 Cemetery gate lodge with bay and central stilt-headed window; Bridlington, Yorkshire; 1879.

109 Bay window with leaded casements; Palmers Green, London; 1920s.

110 Turret window with sash fitting and leaded glazing on upper section; Hampstead, London; c.1890.

111 Steel corner window on semi-detached house; Tufnell Park, London; 1930s.

lawn tennis), rather than just a place for perambulating the shubbery. Since the casement had connotations of cottages and the rural picturesque, leaded lights were frequently revived, particularly when the design included any half-timbered element. A commentator in 1924 wrote: 'Lead lights are, of course, still very popular on account of their picturesque and old-world appearance — few suburban residents have quite forgotten the baronial hall — but in an almost endless repetition of cheap-jack medievalism they defeat their own object, and thus are characteristic only of the present day'. The neo-Georgian look that was also popular in the Edwardian period (led by Edwin Lutyens) returned to the plain sash and even exterior shutters, although it seems unlikely that these were ever used, except on holiday houses.

In direct contrast to the picturesque Arts and Crafts look, where the windows huddled to the centre of the building, in the 1920s windows now moved far into the corners and indeed curved around them. 'Suntrap' windows let as much light as possible into what remained for the most part a traditional, suburban, semi-detached. These developments were crucial to the glass-and-steel building of the Modern Movement. But housing in this style was very rare before 1939 and modernism was more likely to proclaim itself on a suburban house or block of flats through a few eye-catching features. Generous provision of sunlight became a dominating factor in 1950s' buildings. New forms of construction enabled generous glazing and emphasised the view outside, both in blocks of flats and houses where the picture window became a desirable feature.

Bay and bow windows

Both originally medieval forms, bay and bow windows first appeared in the 14th century, but become more frequent during the 15th. A bay window was usually built in relation to the gable. The most significant or prestigious window, a bay or bow, generally related to the great hall and held any valuable stained glass. Ostentatious use of glass was fashionable in the 16th and 17th centuries, so bay windows, and semi-circular bow windows, presented glittering façades. In London the use of bay windows was restricted during the 17th and 18th century because the wood was considered a fire hazard.

Classical Palladian-influenced façades were principally flat apart from the portico, but by the Adam period, many rear elevations were bowed, a feature which subsequently moved round to the front, and became a particular characteristic of Regency style. Carpenters and glaziers became increasingly skilled at glazing and creating sash windows for bows and bays, which also were in demand for new shop fronts. During the Regency period an enthusiasm for sunlight, air and sea views, in resorts such as Brighton and Ramsgate, made such windows very popular.

The canted bay window became almost ubiquitous on terrace housing around 1860, giving each house a more individual feel and expanding the size of the front room. At the turn of the century it was more typical for the bay to be square, and Hermann Muthesius wrote that owing to the inclemency of the British weather bay windows were 'the substitute for seating in the open air...for centuries English architects have shown a special fondness for them'. By the 1920s the suburban bay was given a distinctly modern Art Deco look by curving the walls and extending the windows horizontally. In 20th-century suburban architecture the inclusion of a bay or bow was an important distinction for private house-owners as council or charity-built properties rarely had that extra, expensive dimension.

112 Bay with stone mullion casement windows on manor house: Lytes Cary, Somerset; 1533.

113 Brick bow with stone mullion windows; Burton Agnes Hall, Yorkshire; early 17C.

114 Bay with sash windows decorated in Gothick style; Richmond, Yorkshire; late 18C.

115 Weatherboarded bay with sash windows; Hampstead, London; mid to late 18C.

116 Brick bay with casement windows; Ditcheat, Somerset; late 18C.

117 Bow with sash windows on first floor above shop premises; Winchester, Hampshire; c. 1800.

118 Bow with sash windows on stucco terrace; Brighton, Sussex; c. 1810.

119 Bay with sash windows on stucco terrace; Cheltenham, Gloucestershire; c. 1840–50.

120 Bay with cast-iron casement windows on picturesque cottage; Snitterfield, Warwickshire, c. 1840–50.

121 Thatched bay window added to stone cottage; Stoke Gabriel, Devon; 19C.

Bay and bow windows

122 Bay with Wardian case (1875) on stucco terrace, Kensington, London; 1871.

123 Bay with sash windows on brick terrace with decorated stone frame; Kensington, London; c. 1870.

124 Bay with sash windows on stone terrace with moulded ornament; Bristol; c. 1880s.

125 Bay with sash windows and original external awning fitments on stone terrace; Bath; c. 1880s.

126 Bay with sash window, stone banded in brick; Cardiff; 1903.

127 Bay with sash windows on brick terrace; Hackney, London; c. 1890s.

128 Bay with sash window on stone terrace; Bath; early 20C.

129 Bay with wooden-frame sash window with decorative leaded lights; Walton-on-the-Naze, Essex; early 20C.

130 Bow, wooden-frame casement and transom windows; Evercreech, Somerset; 1930s.

131 Bay with steel-frame suntrap casement windows; Glastonbury, Somerset; 1930s.

132 Stone-frame bow with sash window, top section leaded; Cardiff; 1920s.

Casements and mullions

The casement was the earliest form of fixed window and it remained the norm for cottages and vernacular buildings. The term casement literally refers to the framed section that holds the glass in place, so can also apply to a bow, bay, dormer or oriel. A casement window was hinged at the side and in Britain it generally opened outwards although where there are working shutters it may open inwards. The verticals supporting the casements, which may be stone or wood, are termed mullions. Moulded stone mullions often appear in conjunction with a drip-mould over the top designed to protect the casement from the wet. Casements are unsuitable for large areas of glass and are difficult to use where verticality is the desired effect, hence the popularity of the sash window.

For an upright (rather than a landscape) window a transom (horizontal bar) was added. This may be called a cross-head window. Typically, 20th-century housing had a transom window: the upper section usually opened out from the top and was often separately decorated with coloured glass. To bring maximum light into a house with casement windows several would often be placed in a row: this was a common feature of Arts and Crafts houses and flats. The design of modern steel-framed windows was based on the basic casement type.

The steel-framed window, an essential feature in the glass-and-steel building of the Modern Movement, was the next revolution, introduced around 1920. Its advantages were clear: unlike wood it could fit tightly, it could be ordered in manufactured standard units complete with fittings and pivoting hinges were developed which meant that the whole window could be cleaned from the inside (a particularly important consideration for flat-dwellers). Steel windows did rust, but it was discovered that this could be prevented in the late 1930s by galvanising the entire frame with zinc. The most prominent feature was the horizontally glazed, 'streamlined' metal window (for which Crittall was the principal supplier). Post-war, the mass-produced metal window was as functional and as economical as possible, often reduced to a simple opening casement or side-sliding sash windows in limited sizes.

| 133 | 134 | | 137 | 138 | 139 |
| 135 | 136 | | | 140 | |

133 Timber-mullioned window with leaded casements on timber-frame house; Lavenham, Suffolk; medieval.

134 Wooden-frame cross-head window with casements; Abinger Hammer, Surrey; c. 1660.

135 Stone-mullioned window with drip mould over leaded casements; Martock, Somerset; 17C.

136 Wooden casement set in brick and stone; Knightsbridge, London; c. 1880.

137 Stone-mullioned window with wooden casements; Hopton, Derbyshire.

138 Wooden-frame casement windows, including dormer and bow; Gidea Park, Essex; 1912.

139 Steel casement windows; Twickenham, London; 1930s.

140 Metal casement window, set in concrete frame; Chelmsford, Essex; 1950s.

Sash windows

Primitive sash windows already existed in France, but the sash window that opened smoothly with a system of pulleys and counterweights and that effectively eliminated both draughts and awkward inward or outward openings, was probably a British invention of around 1670, discussed with enthusiasm even at the august level of the Royal Society. Early examples often had segmental or swept-head tops; the glazing bars were relatively thick (two inches) and the panes of glass small, as many as four or five across. Over the next century these were reduced in width and elegantly moulded. There are plenty of exceptions but as a general rule mid-Georgian sash windows had six-over-six, or eight-over-eight panes. Regency and early 19th-century sash windows were usually four-over-four, sometimes with a margin or border or with decorative curved and arched glazing bars. Improved glass manufacture reduced panes to two-over-two, and finally just one large pane over another (a strengthening 'horn' or bracket at the base of each upper frame compensated for the extra weight). Patterned glazing and coloured glass was revived for the top section only on late Victorian and Edwardian sash windows.

Side-sliding sash windows (an unsophisticated version of the form) usually appeared on cottages or village houses. Unlike a proper sash window these did not need the complicated weight-and-pulley mechanism. This pattern was very common in late 20th-century aluminium-frame windows.

141

144   145   146

142   143

147   148

141 Side-sliding sash window; Market Overton, Rutland; 19C.

142 9-on-6-pane unrecessed sash window with internal shutters; Bristol; 1709–11.

143 6-on-6-pane unrecessed sash window with segmental head on terrace; Chelsea, London; mid-18C.

144 2-on-2-pane with margin lights on stucco terrace; Regent's Park, London; c. 1820.

145 Arched sash with margin lights on stucco terrace; Notting Hill, London; c. 1835.

146 4-on-4 pane sash window with separate side lights, stone terrace; Clifton, Bristol; 1820–30.

147 3-on-3-pane sash window on stone cottage; Grasmere, Cumbria; 19C.

148 Coloured glass top section sash window on brick terrace; Holloway, London; 1898.

Classical windows

The Venetian window is tripartite with a central arched window flanked by two straight-headed smaller sidelights. Venetian windows are also called Palladian, even though Palladio was only one among many who used them.

Employed by Donato Bramante and other Italian Renaissance architects the Venetian window was introduced in England in the 17th century. Prior to the general adoption of the sash window the shape also appeared traced on leaded casement windows. By the 1720s the Venetian window was one of the hallmarks of grand Palladian architecture, but it also became one of the most popular motifs of the 18th century, appearing on thousands of ordinary Georgian houses. Isaac Ware described them in 1756 in his *Complete Body of Architecture* as 'calculated for shew, and very pompous in their nature; and when executed with judgement, of extreme elegance'. As the entire triple opening counted as one window the Venetian represented good value for purposes of window taxation. It subsequently appeared in the late 19th and early 20th centuries as one of a range of interesting window shapes, for example as a small hall window beside the front door.

The Diocletian window is named for the ancient Baths of Diocletian in Rome from which the Italian Renaissance architects took their inspiration. Lunette-shaped with two vertical glazing bars, it was nearly always used on top or attic storeys or at basement level.

Circular windows (also called medallion, bull's eye or *œil de bœuf*) appear at the same time, although their shape necessarily limited their use. They were also rather more baroque than suited the general taste, but were perfect for pediments and for use in conjunction with elaborate features such as domes and cupolas. As a quirky shape they appeared erratically at all periods particularly in halls and stairwells.

149 Venetian shape in leaded casement windows; Hadleigh, Suffolk; 1676.

150 Diocletian window above Venetian window; Saltram, Plymouth, Devon; 18C.

151 Double Venetian window; Rokeby Hall, Yorkshire; c.1730.

149

152   153   154

155   156

150

151

157   158

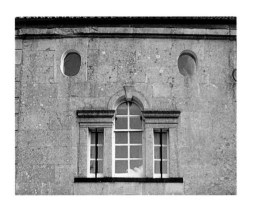

152 Venetian window on gate lodge; Prior Park, Bath; 18C.

153 Venetian windows on town house; Broad Street, Ludlow, Shropshire; c. 1760.

154 Venetian ground-floor hall window on semi-detached; Acton, London; c. 1912.

155 Diocletian windows on estate cottages; Harewood, Yorkshire; late 18C.

156 Neo-Georgian Diocletian window; Hampshire; 1989.

157 Circular window on lodge; Charborough, Dorset; 1790.

158 Neo-Georgian circular window; Holland Park, London; 1950s–1960s.

Dormer and oriel windows

Dormers originally appeared on steep Gothic roofs, but were equally typical on the high roofs of the Classical late 17th century, Queen Anne or early Georgian houses. If a house had a mansard roof, it almost inevitably had dormer windows. Often windows of convenience rather than design, dormers were frequently inserted later, for example in cottages to provide extra height at upper-floor level. They were an economical way of creating an upper floor in a single-storey building and were particularly characteristic of long, low Scottish cottages and bungalows with one upper room. Half-dormers occurred when the window base was in the wall, but the top protruded from the roof. The deep roofs of the Arts and Crafts style frequently incorporated dormer windows.

Most dormers emerged from the roof on a small gable, but there are examples dating from the early 20th century where the roof was curved to create an 'eyebrow' over the top of the window, an effect common in thatch and imitated with tile. A roof-light, by contrast, had the window let into the pitch of the roof.

Oriels (projecting upper-level windows) appeared on both stone and timber-framed medieval houses. Being a prominent feature the oriel window was often decorated with heraldic devices or Gothic ornamentation, and was roofed or surmounted with a castellated or pierced frieze. Usually three-sided, it could also be five-sided. It was often placed in line with the dais in the great hall. Its usefulness as a look-out made the oriel a favourite on gatehouses and lodges. Oriel windows were often made to take advantage of a particular view of sea or landscape

Eighteenth- and 19th-century oriel windows usually had Gothic or Gothic Revival ornamentation in reference to the origin of the form, and were often later additions to the main structure. At the end of the 19th century the oriel was a favourite window in Queen Anne style, stripped of all Gothic associations. Twentieth-century suburban terrace and semi-detached houses also sometimes featured small triangular oriels that conferred added glamour.

159 Oriel window on manor house; Great Chalfield, Wiltshire; late 15C.

160 Dormer window on barns converted to cottages; Arlington Row, Bibury, Gloucestershire; 14C building, 16C/17C dormers.

161 Dormer windows on town house; Salisbury, Wiltshire; late 17C.

162 Gothick-style oriel on brick terrace; Hampstead, London; later addition to house (c.1800).

163 Gothick-style oriel; Cheltenham, Gloucestershire; c.1820–30.

164 Dormer on whitewashed stone cottage; Kirkmichael, Ayrshire; 19C.

165 Half-dormer on stone cottage; Newton-by-the-Sea, Northumberland; 19C.

166 Double-height Arts and Crafts oriels on studio house; Chelsea, London; 1893–94.

167 Arts and Crafts oriel with decorative plasterwork; Hampstead, London; 1895.

168 Dormers on terrace; Port Sunlight, Cheshire; 1890s.

Curious windows

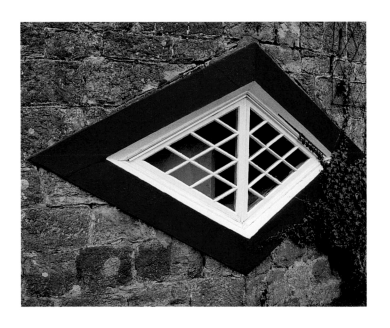

Experimentation with quirkily shaped windows was usually confined to lighting odd spots in houses such as halls, stairwells, attics, or to unconventional polygonal buildings.

Interest in exotic styles, a theme of the late 18th and early 19th centuries, also contributed to the genre, and windows with scalloped or ogee-arched heads appeared styled as 'Hindoo', 'Oriental' or 'Chinese'. Although these were more common in incidental garden buildings they are most likely to appear in frivolous small lodges and gatehouses. The exploration of new ways of building, for example in siting houses underground, present a challenge to find new solutions in window shapes.

169			173	174	175
170	171	172	176		177

169 Wooden-frame window on circular house; A La Ronde, Exmouth, Devon; 1798.

170 Steel window with concrete rustic lintel; Smithfield, London; 1980s.

171 Carved stone basement window; Burford, Oxfordshire; c. 1700.

172 Gable window; Hampstead, London; c.1885.

173 Sash window on brick terrace; Cambridge; c. 1840.

174 Non-opening window on pebbledash brick terrace; East Finchley, London; 1930s.

175 Staircase window; Cirencester, Gloucestershire; early 20C.

176 Window lighting underground house; Tetbury, Gloucestershire; 1990s.

177 Non-opening window with ventilation louvre at base; Haddenham, Buckinghamshire; 1960s.

Glass

Early glass was either blown as a muff-shaped cylinder which was then split lengthwise to produce a sheet or 'brode-glass', or it was spun into discs which came out at roughly four feet in diameter, and was known as crown glass. This method created a central 'bull's-eye' or 'bullion', caused by the removal of the pontil, which was generally discarded or used in less prominent windows. These were purposely produced and used as a decorative feature in the 19th and 20th centuries, either to make the window obscure, or to create a fake Georgian look.

Plate glass was introduced to Britain from France, and made in Lancashire from 1773. Stronger and thicker because it was cast, it was also relatively expensive. Plate glass could also be polished and appear flawless. In the 1880s Chance Brothers introduced sheet glass which was also polished but thinner and cheaper. Combined with the repeal of the glass tax in 1851, expanses of glass could now be used on relatively ordinary houses.

Some of the grandest Tudor houses had sections of coloured and painted glass in their most important windows. Coloured glass, mostly yellow and pale green, was occasionally used in the Regency period along the margins of sash windows and doors.

The Gothic Revival was a catalyst for the reappraisal of stained glass. Coloured glass was thought suitable for prominent places, such as front-door panels, halls and staircase windows. The individual feature of the (often circular) coloured window remained a defining characteristic of suburban houses well into the 1920s.

Glass bricks were originally developed to let light into basement workshops and stores from the street above, but were not used on domestic buildings until the 1930s. They were also a secure way of letting light into halls and stairwells.

Technological developments in the second half of the 20th century expanded the opportunities for using glass in domestic architecture. for example as picture windows, 'curtain' walls, and in ecologically designed housing.

178   179   182   183   184

180   181   185   186   187

178 Great Hall window of leaded panes in manor house; Trerice, Cornwall; 1570s.

179 Heraldic glass; Haddon Hall, Derbyshire; 16C.

180 Crown glass window; Widdicombe, Devon; 18C/early 19C.

181 Pane of bottle-glass in cottage window; Coggeshall, Essex; 18C/19C.

182 Glazed porch with acid-etched decoration and cut red glass; Brighton, Sussex; mid 19C.

183 Painted and stained glass; Broadstairs, Kent; c. 1870.

184 Stained glass front door; Cardiff; c. 1920.

185 Glass bricks on stairwell to flats; Camden, London; 1930s.

186 Front door and wall in glass; Hampstead, London; 1975.

187 Glass brick façade; Islington, London; 1994.

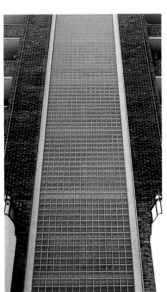

Glazing patterns

Window glazing bars made up in a rich variety of geometric shapes, and frets were deemed a suitable addition to the Gothick- or Chinoiserie-style buildings that appeared sporadically throughout the second half of the 18th century. The Regency period continued this interest in exotic styles. A rich variety of glazing patterns emerged during the first decades of the 19th century. Arched sash windows on terrace housing showed interesting combinations of curves and circles, details often echoed on the front door or fanlight. Fancy glazing was almost *de rigueur* for the picturesque cottage or *cottage orné*, and could be made up quite cheaply in cast iron in a wide range of lozenges, diamonds and bands that were far more resilient than leaded glazing.

Most ordinary housing of the mid-19th century had newly affordable large panes of glass, but at the end of the century the wheel of fashion turned again and elaborately glazed windows re-emerged. The architect M. Hugh Baillie Scott's instructions were typical: 'The beauty of glass depends entirely on its use in small pieces, in a setting which will make them sparkle and twinkle. The large sheet with its vacant stare, should never be used unless under stress of circumstances'. These windows also signalled expensive ornamentation — the builder's added value — and some were used in conjunction with coloured and painted glass windows and door lights; decorative glazing was often confined to the top one-third of the total window space. In the 20th century lead glazing was used to produce an 'old-worlde' appearance and to suggest craftsmanship. For example, the diamond pane was used in tandem with Mock-Tudor half-timbered ornamentation.

188 Cast-iron casement windows; Martock, Somerset; mid-19C.

189 Wooden glazing bars on Gothick-style sash window; Stout's Hill, Uley, Gloucestershire; 1743.

190 Wooden glazing bars on Indian- or Oriental-style sash window; Brighton, Sussex; 1830.

191 Wooden glazing bars on sash window; Clifton, Bristol; mid-19C.

192 Wooden glazing bars on Gothick-style oriel window; Farnham, Surrey; early 19C.

193 Pointed window on *cottage orné* lodge; Oakhill, Somerset; c. 1790.

194 Cast-iron casement windows; Bitton, Gloucestershire; c. 1840.

195 Leaded glazing on oriel window of *cottage orné*; Old Warden, Bedfordshire; c. 1840.

196 Cast-iron casement window on lodge; Holkham, Norfolk; c. 1840.

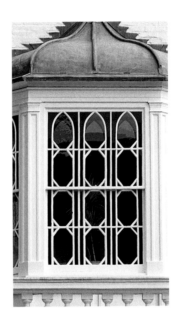

Balconies and verandas

A stone balustrade cantilevered out from a first-floor window was a typically Classical form that appeared occasionally on grand houses in the 17th century. This style was more associated with fashion than utility since balconies were rarely a natural choice in the British climate. Hermann Muthesius described them as 'lifeless appendages', considering the bay window to be the British alternative. Nevertheless, from the 1770s onwards, ironwork balconies became almost ubiquitous on terrace housing. They were designed either as single balconies fronting first-floor windows (and providing a safety guard), or ran continuously along the terrace providing both a practical fire escape and a place for a few plants.

Balconies, along with verandas (the same motif but at ground level) were a key feature of Regency style, and both frequently featured a scallop-edged canopy of copper or zinc. A canopied balcony of this period is often referred to as a Trafalgar balcony. This was also the moment when the British discovered the seaside and the sea-view, and indeed balconies have remained an essential part of British seaside architecture. Balconies were most in demand for flat-dwellers and were usually incorporated into the design of both mansion flats and artisan blocks. They were a space to take the air, grow a few plants (Victorian garden literature contains many references to 'window gardening'), and a convenient place to dry washing in the absence of a communal drying green or garden.

At the turn of the 20th century sleeping outside was considered highly desirable, and some houses in garden cities and suburbs were designed with 'sleeping balconies'. Capitalising on the benefits of maximum sun and air was a central tenet of the Modern Movement and as much balcony space, roof terrace and open-air walkways were incorporated into flat design as possible. The veranda on a bungalow was equally designed to encourage outdoor living.

197 Iron balcony with palmette motif; Adam Street, London; c. 1768.

198 Iron balconies and canopies on terrace; Cheltenham, Gloucestershire; c. 1815–20.

199 Continuous balcony along terrace; New Town, Edinburgh; 1820s.

200 Iron balconies and canopies facing the sea; Royal Crescent, Brighton, Sussex; 1798–1807.

201 Canopied iron balcony; Holborn, London; c. 1805–10.

202 Continuous iron balcony across front of house; Bath; c. 1810.

203 Canopied iron balcony on bow-fronted house; Bath; c. 1810.

204 Iron veranda; Pwllheli, Gwynedd; c.1820.

205 Canopied iron balcony on bow-fronted house; Brighton, Sussex; c. 1820–25.

197		200	201	202
198				
199		203	204	205

Balconies and verandas

206 Iron balconies on model dwellings; Shoreditch, London; 1860–62.

207 Iron balconies on mansion flats; Westminster, London; c. 1890.

208 Stone and iron balconies on flats; Kensington, London; 1898.

209 Iron and wood balcony off bedroom; Cardiff; c. 1900.

210 Brick and concrete balconies on flats; Ealing, London; c. 1935.

211 Concrete balconies on Modern Movement block of flats; Highgate, London; 1936–38.

212 Brick balconies on flats; Chelsea, London; 1952.

| 206 | 207 | 208 | | 212 | 213 | | 214 |
| 209 | 210 | 211 | | 215 | 216 | 217 | 218 |

213 Concrete and steel balconies on walk-up block of flats; Stevenage New Town, Hertfordshire; 1955–57.

214 Wooden balconies with metal struts on self-build terrace; Lewisham, London; 1970s.

215 Balconies on concrete tower block, public housing; Notting Hill, London; 1973.

216 Glass and brick balconies on flats; St John's Wood, London; late 1960s/early 1970s.

217 Slatted wood balconies and walkways; Byker Wall, Newcastle-on-Tyne; 1970s.

218 Metal balconies on housing trust (Peabody) flats; Sutton, Surrey; 2002.

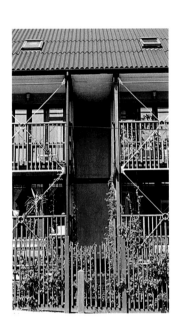

Stone

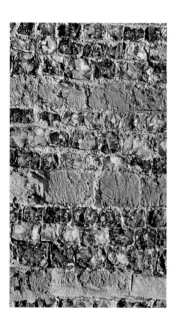

Building in stone has always been prestigious, reflecting the amount of effort involved in producing a stone wall (far greater than timber-framing or brick). As a building material, stone has the advantage of being recyclable, as lintels, carvings, door and window frames were often re-used from one building to the next. Most stone houses in Britain have been built from whatever was locally quarried, giving domestic architecture an immense range of colours and textures. In brief the main types are:

Limestone (specific names include Portland, Ham, Colleyweston, Bath, Kentish rag, but also includes chalk and lias. Chalk as a building stone is sometimes referred to as clunch). This occurs in bands stretching from the south-west to the north-east. Some is very good for carving and it is used for both walls and roofing.

Sandstone (includes Yorkshire gritstone, Horsham, Red sandstone, carstone greensand and millstone grit) varies in colour and is quarried patchily all over Britain. Available in much larger blocks than limestone, it cannot however be carved to the same crispness.

Granite is the hardest building stone and therefore most difficult to work. It is used particularly in north-eastern Scotland, Cornwall and Cumbria.

Flints occur in chalk and are used mainly in East Anglia and in southern coastal areas where there is little other local stone. They are used in their natural cobble shape or split (knapped) and sometimes squared, and because of their size have to be used with brick or stone for corner-building.

Other forms include *pudding-stone* (a natural aggregate); *slate* from north-west and mid-Wales, the Lake District and Cornwall, which splits into slabs and tiles and was thus only suitable for roofing and cladding. There is virtually no *marble* present in Britain, but the description is given to extremely hard limestone such as *Purbeck marble*.

219 Banded limestone and flint; Maiden Newton, Dorset.

220 Knapped flint; Beccles, Suffolk.

221 Sandstone with granite snecking; Port William, Dumfries and Galloway.

222 Granite; Leith, Edinburgh.

223 Sandstone; Dumfries, Dumfries and Galloway.

224 Carstone with galletting; Denver, Norfolk.

225 Lias limestone with ammonite; Evercreech, Somerset.

226 Flint cobbles and painted brick; Brighton, Sussex.

227 Ashlar limestone; Woodchester, Gloucestershire.

228 Reconstituted stone; Uley, Gloucestershire; 1992.

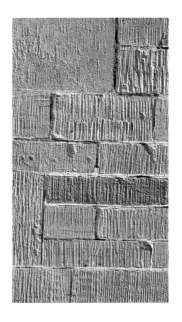

Stone carving

Carved stone detail was used to express quality and prestige, and to create fashion in architectural style. It has also been used to personalise a house by the addition of carved stone gate piers with heraldic devices and crests, and by plaques with initials and dates. The skills of early stonemasons were honed on churches, but many motifs could also be found in domestic architecture: masks, corbel stones, finials or gothic tracery. Builders during the Tudor and Jacobean period were passionately addicted to ornamentation and included as much carving as possible anywhere that it would fit, as finials, labels, or cresting. By contrast, 17th- and 18th-century Classicism designated specific areas for carved ornament: capitals on columns and pilasters, door and window surrounds, pediments, quoins, rustication and keystones. Isaac Ware warned: 'Take care in proportion, or they cease to be ornaments: they are loads and patches upon the face of the building, and seem not to belong'.

During the 19th century the increased use of steam saws, hammers and mobile cranes made stone a far more accessible commodity. The Gothic Revival, combined with mechanisation, led to an explosion of carved decoration, much of it in the naturalistic tradition. Quarries supplied sections of carved stone for window frames, balustrades, cornices, doorways and porches that could be ordered from their catalogues. Victorian builders' catalogues also advertised a number of artificial stones such as Ransome's Patent Concrete Stone (an 'admixture of sand and chalk with silicate of soda pressed into moulds or blocks and afterwards saturated with a solution of chloride of calcium'), Patent Victoria Stone, or Syenitic Stone. Materials such as these were made into gate finials, urns, balustrades or ornamental door or window heads. By the end of World War I superfluous stone ornament had become both unfashionable and economically unviable.

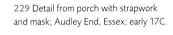

229 Detail from porch with strapwork and mask; Audley End, Essex; early 17C.

230 Grotesque head keystone over sash window; Bristol; 1709–11.

231 Vermiculated rustication on gatehouse; Fonthill, Tisbury, Wiltshire; mid-18C.

232 Entablature and Corinthian capital; Queen Square, Bath; 1728.

233 Carved doorcase; Queen Square, Bath; c. 1730.

234 Entablature and emblem; The Circus, Bath; 1754.

235 Porch and decorated window surround; Sherborne, Dorset; late 18C.

236 House name plaque with date and owner's initials; Evercreech, Somerset; 1899.

237 Keystone on doorway; Cardiff; c. 1900.

238 Frieze of trees on block of flats; Marylebone, London; 1903.

Stone houses

239 Boulder-built longhouse, farmhouse and byre; Rhydymain, Gwynedd.

240 Millstone grit weavers' houses; Saddleworth, Yorkshire.

241 Granite cottage with sandstone dressings; Kennethmont, Aberdeenshire.

242 Picturesque limestone cottage; Oakhill, Somerset.

243 Farmhouse; Newstead, Yorkshire.

244 Ashlar sandstone; Alyth, Perthshire.

245 Limestone house and porch; Bibury, Gloucestershire.

246 Limestone chequered with brick; Stockton, Wiltshire.

247 Ashlar limestone; Oundle, Northamptonshire.

248 Flint with white brick; Mildenhall, Suffolk.

249 Sandstone farmhouse; Hawnby, Yorkshire.

250 Chalk (or clunch) with brick; Burnham Overy, Norfolk.

251 Flint banded with red brick; Bulford, Wiltshire.

239

240

241

244

245 246

247 248

242 243 249 250 251

Datestones

Datestones appear on all sorts of housing in all periods, ingeniously worked in brick, moulded in plaster, carved in stone and incised in wood. Dates were often combined with the initials of the house-builder or first owner, or two sets of initials marked a wedding and perhaps the beginning of the owners' life in the house. Dates were particularly common on estate cottages, designating the periods during which the landowner improved the lot of his tenant. Equally model housing and dwelling houses were frequently dated. Very early dates are likely to be optimistic suppositions or results of researching by subsequent owners and are not necessarily contemporaneous with the building. New wings and additions were similarly marked. Some years are more 'date conscious' than others, for example Queen Victoria's Golden and Diamond Jubilee years, 1887 and 1897, frequently appear.

252 Painted relief plasterwork; Totnes, Devon; 1585.

253 Painted carved stone door lintel; Askham, Cumbria; 1674.

254 Painted stone label on lintel; Falkland, Fife; 1721.

255 Date and monogram carved on pediment; Bristol; 1747.

256 Keystone; Painswick, Gloucestershire; 1800.

257 Iron plaque on terrace; Elsecar, Yorkshire; 1837.

258 Plaster date plaque on semi-detached villa; St John's Wood, London; 1847.

259 Date over entrance to flats; Chelsea, London; 1886.

260 Albert Terrace; Holt, Norfolk; 1887.

261 Stone carved datestone; Wincanton, Somerset; 1891.

262 Terracotta panels; Tottenham, London; 1892.

263 Date in mortar on brick; St Osyth, Essex; 1911.

264 Painted gable on terrace; Acton, London; 1912.

265 Moulded concrete datestone at base of outside gate; Kentish Town, London; 1987.

252			257	258	259
253	254	255	260	261	262
256			263	264	265

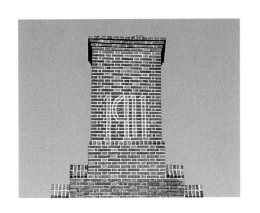

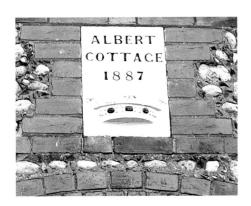

Doors

266 Principal doorway surmounted by heraldic escutcheon; Montacute House, Somerset; 1590s.

267 Pair of carved wooden canopies; City of London; 1703.

268 Carved, initialled and dated lintel stone; Grewelthorpe, Yorkshire; 1706.

269 Carved stone motto on courtier's house with date and builder's marks ('Contentment is Great Riches'); Falkland, Fife; 1607.

If any aspect of a house is going to have ornamental detail lavished upon it, the most favoured candidate is the principal entrance where maximum impact can be made. It is also the part of the house that is most susceptible to alteration, either from aspirations to keep up with changing fashions or from the practical reasons of general wear and tear. Regional differences are most apparent in door design.

Relatively few medieval houses were grand enough to have a decorated front entrance, and those that did were almost inevitably stone-built. As with ecclesiastical building, domestic doors saw the round-headed Anglo-Norman arch, pointed Gothic arch, segmental arch and ogee arch follow in succession, in some cases elaborated with carved decoration. Early doors were probably no more than vertical planks, strengthened horizontally at the back and hung on iron strap hinges, sometimes with nail patterns along the boarding. Individuality might be expressed through ornamental shaping or incised patterns on the hinges. Any decorative treatment of the wood itself could reflect the prevailing style in furniture and panelling, for example linen-fold panelling or Gothic arcading. But it seems probable that doors were by and large serviceable and secure. The basic planked door remained the norm for most ordinary cottage doors, back doors and service doors.

The door frames most characteristic of the late 15th and 16th centuries were either a shallow segmental arch or, increasingly, a rectangular lintel, and this was the spot for datestones, builders' names, mason's marks or a carved label or strap. The Jacobeans loved elaborate panelling and moulding and applied it to front doors, but by the late 17th and early 18th century panels had been simplified and usually reduced to six or eight per door, with the smallest panels at the top and bottom.

An increasing awareness of Classicism was the impetus for a complete change in the style of doors. Renaissance architects had designed doorways like temple fronts, topping them with pediment or cornice and flanking them with columns. This was a key element from the Classical vocabulary that could be quickly absorbed, and from around the 1680s new doorcase designs appeared. They fell into two basic shapes: a projecting flat cornice supported on two carved console brackets, or more elaborate designs for example an arched pediment (segmental or swan-neck pediment) and coved arched hoods typically carved with a shell. Individual woodcarvers and stonemasons filled in the detail with a variety of motifs favoured during the period, such as acanthus scrolls, winged cherub heads, or swags of fruit and flowers. Triangular pediments superseded these types by the mid-18th century.

A feature of the Classical house was a ground or semi-basement service floor below a raised main reception floor, (the idea of the piano nobile taken from Renaissance architecture). This necessitated a flight of steps, often elegantly splaying out at ground level and bordered by a balustrade or iron railing, which led up to the main entrance, emphasising its importance. The steps up to the front door, even if reduced to two or three, remained a marker for a house of substance throughout much of the 19th century. Such steps in the same period were built straight up and usually led to a columned portico, which in turn might support a balcony or balustrade. For the inhabitants of working-class terraces the significance of keeping the door step clean and white was a measure of respectability and good housekeeping when there was little other ornament attached to the front door.

Numerous pattern books offered builders and craftsmen even in remote parts of Britain a range of options, even if some were distinctly unfashionable by the time they had been published, copied and possibly pirated. James Gibbs's *Book of Architecture containing Designs of Buildings and Ornaments* (1728) introduced the distinctive exaggerated blocking around doorcases (and windows to match) which was used well past the middle of the century and appeared in various versions in later pattern books. Isaac Ware in his *Complete Body of Architecture* (1756) gave a clear idea of the importance of the design of the principal door and the need to build it correctly: '(We) shall recommend the care of it to the architect's most serious thought. If any error is committed, it is obvious to the first eye that is cast upon the building; and it is an unlucky one, for this reason, that will put the vulgar in mind of the builder's stumbling at the threshold of his undertaking'.

As the 18th century progressed, so did the prevalence of the arched door frame, at first set under a triangular pediment, in conjunction with columns or pilasters (usually Ionic or Doric rather than Corinthian, as the former were thought suitably robust for an exterior). The semi-circle created a space for the fanlight thus allowing light into the hallway. Arched fanlights were so popular that by the 1770s the decorative carved wood or stone doorcase was disappearing leaving the focus on the elaborate fanlight pattern. A contributing factor to this change in fashion was probably building regulations that increasingly restricted the amount of flammable wood allowed on façades. In place of the door frame the entrance was emphasised, on brick buildings, with stucco and Coade stone by means of a variety of decorated keystones, rusticated blocks and quoins.

By the Regency period, straightforward panelling had become less popular. Instead there was an enthusiasm for strongly vertical designs with decorative studding and circular bull's-eye panels: Greek Revival touches such as incised linear decoration or reeding were motifs that as usual simultaneously appeared on furniture. Where the single-arched ground-floor window appeared on early 19th-century terraces, the door panels and the window glazing sometimes shared a common motif, but thereafter the four-panel door became ubiquitous. Any suggestion of the door being 'framed' had more or less disappeared, unless by a porch or portico, which were increasingly popular. Clearly there was a need to offer the visitor some element of shelter at the front door, and with the increasing use of wrought- and cast-iron, this could be provided by light ironwork porches or, in terrace housing, by a continuous balcony running along at first-floor level. Balconies and verandas shielded the house from light and, to compensate, glazing in doors and the hybrid door/window (the French window) were introduced.

Victorian architecture favoured more complicated doors, although detail and ornament were in no way confined to door entrances and tended to cover the entire building. The revival of the gable led naturally to the resurrection of the porch as an important feature while the front door itself tended to disappear from view. Indeed the asymmetry of the style meant that the front door was no longer necessarily the most immediately obvious central element on the façade of a house. Ornament had become relatively cheap: it was now possible to have granite pillars, a gabled porch, polychrome brick trim, stained-glass door-lights, patterned encaustic ceramic tiled floor and naturalistic Gothic foliage sprouting from the columns and colonettes. Names and numbers of houses became increasingly relevant and were prominently marked. The place for the name of the house or number was gilded or painted on the door-light (or porch or portico), or carved in stone or plaster above the door. A much-loved feature of Victorian life and ornamentation was the motto. Possibly only in this period could 'God's Providence is Mine Inheritance' be primly carved over the front door or, more sportively on a hunting box, a motto such as 'Fay ce Voudras' [Do as you will].

Ornament, on blocks of model dwellings or lodgings, was usually confined to the entrance doorway. This was often used to proclaim the charitable body who had funded the building and, for practical reasons, to make the door as conspicuous as possible since shared entrances were common. Any costs incurred by this ornamentation were usually minimal. A common practice from the second half of the 19th century until the late 20th century on blocks of public and worker housing such as this was for individual doors to lead off open exterior 'corridors' built at every level, sometimes with ironwork railings, brick walls or panelling. On the other hand, a mansion block used its entrance as a clear signal that, although it might be the same shape and scale as working-class lodgings, the building was intended for a different class of inhabitant. This was demonstrated by elaborately ornamented entrances, bevelled and cut-glass door-lights, carved doors and elaborate ceramic walling which would reflect the amount of money spent on the building. Late 19th-century maisonettes were identified by a pair of doors within the same porch, each leading to a separate floor.

The fashion for building in red brick during the period of Queen Anne Revival meant that once

270 Doors on terrace housing for workers at Courtauld's; Halstead, Essex; c. 1900.

271 Plate glass and ironwork door; Highgate, London; late 1950s/1960s.

again there was an emphasis on the framing of the door: big, deep doorcases with elaborate pediments, and gables with cut and rubbed brick ornament; swags of fruit and flowers hanging on pediments; ornamental panels, typically depicting pots of lilies or sunflowers flanking either side of the door. On houses like this, by and large substantial, detached and in the suburbs, doors were elaborately panelled, carved and glazed in a variety of designs which could be chosen from the extensive manufacturers' trade catalogues.

In the design of typically Arts and Crafts-inspired houses the front door was often recessed back from the façade within a wide entrance arch. Characteristically the doors themselves reverted to simple planking or tongue-and-groove. Door furniture was given a hand-wrought iron look rather than made in shiny brass.

During this period most doors also had some glass panels to let light into the hall but retain privacy. The glass was therefore designed to be semi-opaque: often either patterned glass or panes of greenish 'bottle' glass. Coloured-glass door-lights were extremely popular and the top two (of four) door panels were often replaced with panes of painted and coloured glass. Door decoration presented an easy opportunity for bringing the house up-to-date: Gothic quatrefoils and fleurs de lys, naturalistic birds and flowers, Edwardian wreaths, Art Nouveau plant forms or Art Deco chevrons. Coloured glass panels in front doors stayed in favour with suburban houses well into the 1930s, as a feature that denoted expenditure and proclaimed individuality. For example, heraldry and galleons possibly conveyed a feeling of security, referring back to a supposedly golden age for inhabitants of a mock Tudor house.

While a large proportion of the population still had servants, it was considered necessary to have a separate entrance which led straight into the kitchen for servants and for tradesmen's deliveries. This would either be the back door or the door in the basement area which was always utilitarian in design, and often involved a separate path and gate. When both servants and deliveries went into decline after the Second World War more thought was given to the design of the back door and utilities.

By the 20th century people expected far more light and possibly less privacy. As usual doors followed the fashionable angles and proportions — for example Art Deco verticals or sunray patterns. By the 1950s the majority of the door area was now glazed, made possible by the production of toughened glass. In some cases the glass was framed in metal which set no limitations on the design. Alternatively, doors were entirely flush, without any suggestion of moulding or panelling, and glazing was often reduced to a geometric circle or square. Post-war houses in the 1950s and 1960s frequently featured a long glass panel (or hall window) down to floor level beside the front door. At the start of the 21st century, an increased sensitivity towards security issues dealt a blow to the fashion for transparency and favoured a return to a more fortified look.

Vernacular and early doors

272 Stone fragments of Norman church door frame on 19C cottage; Sherborne, Gloucestershire.

273 Linenfold panelling on courtyard doors; Paycocke's, Coggeshall, Essex; c. 1500.

274 Planked door with repair scarfed in at base and strap hinges; Burford, Oxfordshire; stone arched opening 15C/16C.

275 Boarded door with filleted joints on manor house; Great Chalfield, Wiltshire; late 15C/early 16C.

276 Wooden lintel and planked door; Arlington Row, Bibury, Oxfordshire; 14C barns converted to cottages in 17C.

277 Wide planked door with base repairs; Sutton Courtenay, Oxfordshire; 17C.

| 272 | 273 | 274 | | 278 | 279 | 280 |
| 275 | 276 | 277 | | 281 | 282 | 283 |

278 Panelled door, dated; Burton Constable Hall, East Riding, Yorkshire; 1601.

279 Doorcase with shell hood, pargetted ornament above; Newport, Essex; 1692.

280 Cottage door with horseshoe nailed on wooden lintel; Asthall, Oxfordshire.

281 Cottage door with stone lintel, jambs and steps; Slaidburn, Lancashire.

282 Tongue-and-groove boarded door under stone canopy; Taynton, Oxfordshire.

283 Tongue-and-groove boarded door, estate cottage with ceramic number; Blickling, Norfolk.

18th-century doors

284 Painted carved shell-headed doorcase, 6-panelled door; Bampton, Oxfordshire; early 18C.

285 Carved wooden canopy door; Westminster, London; 1704.

286 Carved stone doorcase with broken pediment canopy and segmental-headed door; Uley, Gloucestershire; early 18C.

287 Stone segmental pediment doorcase with columns, 12-panelled door; Lancaster; 1720s.

288 Canopy doorcase on terrace; Westminster, London; late 1720s.

289 Wood segmental pediment doorcase with spiral columns, 10-panelled door; King's Lynn, Norfolk; early 18C.

| 284 | 285 | 286 | 290 | 291 | 292 |
| 287 | 288 | 289 | 293 | 294 | 295 |

290 Pedimented doorcase with rusticated or Gibbs surround, 4-panelled door; Bury St Edmunds, Suffolk; mid-18C.

291 Doorcase with fluted columns and pediment; Hatfield, Hertfordshire; mid-18C.

292 Doorcase with pediment and fanlight; Nantwich, Cheshire; c. 1790.

293 Six-panelled door with lights (probably inserted later); Chilcombe, Dorset; second half of 18C.

294 Arched doorway with fanlight on terrace; Islington, London; 1786.

295 Six-panelled door with sidelights and fanlight, set within rusticated arch; Charlotte Square, New Town, Edinburgh; 1791.

19th-century doors

296 Arched doorcase with fanlight on terrace; Clapton, London; c. 1820.

297 Stucco doorway in Egyptian style with obelisks and sphinxes; Islington, London; c. 1830.

298 Gothic Revival stucco doorway, with pierced quatrefoil lights; Islington, London; 1838–45.

299 Gothic Revival stone porch; Hackney, London; mid 19C.

300 Brick terrace door with stone lintel and keystone; Southwold, Suffolk; c. 1860–70.

301 Boarded door with decorative Gothic Revival ironwork; North Oxford; 1870s.

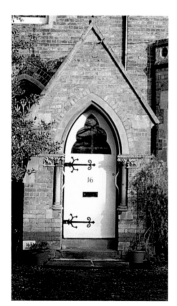

302 Stone doorcase with incised decoration; Morningside, Edinburgh; c. 1870.

303 Glasgow School doorcase with mosaic decoration on artists' house; Kirkcudbright, Dumfries and Galloway; c. 1890.

304 Door with stained glass panel, granite-pillared porch; Fulham, London; late 19C/early 20C.

305 Arched doorway encompassing door and hall oriel window; Hampstead, London; late 19C/early 20C.

306 Entrance to mansion block; Maida Vale, London; c.1890–1900.

307 Brick and pebbledash terrace; Port Sunlight, Cheshire; late 19C/early 20C.

20th-century doors

308 Entrance to small block of flats, dated keystone; Chelsea, London; 1911.

309 Suburban semi-detached door, galleon under full sail in stained-glass panel; Colchester, Essex; 1920s.

310 Arched door and sidelights; Highgate, London; late 1920s.

311 Rendered brick door surround; Gidea Park, Essex; 1934.

312 Entrance to block of flats in stone and brick; Highgate, London; 1934.

313 Art Deco ironwork against glass door; Hendon, London; 1930s.

314 Concrete canopy and glass side-lights on public housing; Islington, London; 1950s.

315 Terrace housing; Bankside, London; 1980s.

316 Flush door on entrance to small block of flats; Bloomsbury, London; early 1990s.

317 Entrance to small block of flats; Limehouse, London; c. 2000.

318 Terrace house in housing association (Guinness Trust); Frome, Somerset; late 1990s.

319 Security door on terrace house refurbished into flats; Camden, London; late 1990s.

Fanlights

The arched opening, whether for doors or windows, was one of the most easily assimilated elements of Classicism, and a radiating pattern was the most obvious way of decorating the space. The fanlight, set under a triangular, pedimented doorcase, became one of the most ubiquitous features of the mid-18th century, and cabinet-makers created inventive rococo patterns for the glazing bars. Early examples from the 1720s looked chunky as the radiating pattern was either fretted out of solid timber, carved, or produced by placing an ironwork grill in front of the glass. Some designs were published, for example in John Crunden's pattern book *Modern or Ornamental Door Tops* (1770) which illustrated both fan-shaped and rectangular windows. An early instance of home improvement, fanlights were often inserted into earlier doors.

The fanlight is closely associated with the style of the Adam Brothers who translated the Venetian or Palladian window most precisely into the door form by emphasising the arch over the door and taking away any pediments. In addition they included lintel-to-floor side-lights, which allowed the fanlight to be far larger, and become the principal ornamental feature of the doorway. Much greater delicacy of fanlight ornament was achieved by the use of very slim glazing bars as well as cast lead, brass or composition motifs soldered onto the exterior of the glass. Ingenious alternative patterns were placed above doors on flat-fronted terrace housing well into the 19th century. Regency fanlights were often composed of concentric circles and loops, and increasingly the lights were rectangular.

Today, the easy availability of 'off-the-shelf Georgian' dropped fanlight doors has meant the loss of thousands of original and more interesting features.

320 Gothick doorcase with matching fanlight tracery and panelling; Gloucester; late 18C.

321 Canopy doorcase with wooden fanlight; Holborn, London; 1730s.

322 Fanlight under pediment, wooden glazing bars; Farnham, Surrey; mid-18C.

323 Elliptical door opening with side-lights; Hampstead, London; late 18C.

324 Pedimented doorcase with fanlight incorporating lantern fitting; Clifton, Bristol; 18C doorcase, early 19C fanlight.

325 Rectangular fanlight with metal glazing bars; Hammersmith, London; late 18C.

326 Arched doorcase with metal glazing bars; Salisbury, Wiltshire; late 18C.

327 Arched doorcase with fanlight and side-lights; Bloomsbury, London; 1776–86.

328 Arched door opening with fanlight; Islington, London; c. 1840.

Porches

For practical reasons the porch has always been seen as more of a necessity in the country. Traditionally it was a place where people could wait to be let into the house. At its simplest it consisted of slabs of stone to keep the rain off the door, and at its most complex the porch was a weatherproof space used for a multitude of purposes, providing a buffer between inside and out. Porches served to retain warmth inside the house as well as providing a neutral zone where deliveries could be safely left or collections made. During the 16th and 17th centuries the gabled porch was a significant feature, often built to double height with a decorative window above the entrance.

One early 19th-century author wrote that a vicarage should be built 'with an open porch as a welcome to the poor' (P. F. Robinson, *Village Architecture*), and this detail was certainly frequently seen as an extension of the hospitality of the house as well as a practical adjunct.

Cottage porches may seem to be a picturesque cliché but they were frequently essential places to work, offering shelter and a light area in a cottage that was often dark and cold. They were usually made from local materials, thatched or tiled, often consciously rustic using rough poles rather than sawn timber. One of the enduring porch patterns, the trellis — in wood, wire-work or ironwork — had a practical application as a support for climbing plants. William Morris built deep sitting porches at Red House in Bexleyheath, facing into the garden, as places to talk and sew.

The porch was an important feature of the suburban house, a way of emphasizing individuality and identifying it as a move away from the featureless urban terrace. At the turn of the 20th century, rather than an outwards projection, the porch space tended to be recessed in from the façade.

| 329 | 330 | | 333 | 334 | 335 |
| 331 | 332 | | 336 | 337 | 338 |

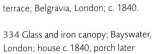

329 Double-storey gabled timber-frame porch; Potterne, Wiltshire; late 15C.

330 Double-storey gabled brick porch; Abinger Hammer, Surrey; c. 1660.

331 Ironwork porch on stone house; Corton, Wiltshire; early 19C.

332 Rustic woodwork porch with twig mosaic; Stedham, Sussex; 19C.

333 Stucco porch creating balcony on terrace; Belgravia, London; c. 1840.

334 Glass and iron canopy; Bayswater, London; house c.1840, porch later addition.

335 Covered-in porch with coloured glass and slate roof on row of cottages; Kingsbridge, Devon; late 19C.

336 Wood and brick porch with coloured glass and house name in gable; Clapham, London; 1890s.

337 Weatherboarded double-storey porch on terrace; Hampstead Garden Suburb, London; 1909.

338 Brick and glass porch; Stevenage New Town, Hertfordshire; 1955–57.

Door furniture

Until the end of the 18th century door furniture (knobs, handles, knockers or locks) would have been made of iron or wood or, if extremely grand, bronze. Doors were either barred and bolted from the inside or fitted with box- or rim-locks fixed to the inside of the door, which opened with large unwieldy keys; however these were extremely easy to pick. Two inventors solved this problem: Joseph Bramah patented a mortise lock in 1784, followed by Jeremiah Chubb in 1818, both producing improved and more impenetrable locks using smaller keys. Later in the century the American Linus Yale patented various locks with small, flat keys which he manufactured from 1868 onwards.

As horse-drawn traffic of the 18th century created muddy and dirty roads, Robert Adam included a cast-iron boot scraper (incorporating his favourite anthemion motif) on one of the houses of his Adelphi development in around 1770. Boot scrapers became a fairly standard feature, often inserted into the wall beside the front door or fixed into the doorstep. In towns and cities before street lighting, iron snuffers were fixed beside the door for link boys to extinguish their torches on arrival.

Brass knockers started appearing in the late 18th century as casting techniques improved. Fashionable motifs included gryphons, female masks, lion's heads or sphinxes. Characteristic Victorian motifs include the woman's hand and the fox mask. Bells tended to supplant knockers from the 1830s onwards when brass or iron bell pushes or pulls appeared beside front door.

Although the Penny Post was introduced in 1840, the need for letter-boxes was not felt for about forty years by which time the volume of post had grown enormously — augmented by the introduction of the Christmas card, postcard and Valentine — and the postman no longer had time to knock on each door to deliver the mail.

339 Wrought ironwork knocker and strap hinge; Coggeshall, Essex.

340 Cast iron bootscraper in anthemion and paw-foot motifs; Westminster, London; 1770s.

341 Snuffer for extinguishing link boys' torches; Bath; late 18C/early 19C.

342 Brass keyhole and door handle; Salisbury, Wiltshire; early 19C.

343 Brass knocker of female mask; Bath; early 19C pattern.

344 Brass bells for 'Servants' and 'Visitors' fixed on gateposts on terrace; Kensington, London; late 19C.

345 Brass vertical letterbox; Hadleigh, Suffolk; late 19C/early 20C.

346 Cast iron fox mask doorknocker on cottage; Holkham, Norfolk; late 19C/early 20C.

347 Lyre knocker; Warwick, Warwickshire; 19C.

348 Cast-iron handle-cum-knocker; Alyth, Perthshire; 19C.

Names and numbers

In 1765 a bill was passed which required newly built streets to be named and houses numbered. The display of door numbers on all houses became mandatory in London in 1805. On estate villages the cottages were often numbered regardless of position, simply to identify them, and were given plain white ceramic number labels on the door.

In rural communities houses and farms had historically been verbally defined by names which related to their purpose, their ownership, their geography or local landmarks (e.g. Wood Hall, Windmill Farm). The sentimental naming of houses appears to be a notion of the picturesque: Blaise Hamlet built in 1812 had Jessamine, Rose, Vine and Sweet Briar Cottages. Names such as Woodcot introduced the idea of the cottage. The idea became far more elaborate as the century progressed. By using the definite article a suggestion of grandeur was conferred (e.g. The Elms, The Towers). Victorian Gothic Revival houses were frequently given names which suggested antiquity such as The Chantry or The Grange, and such names frequently appear cut into the gate piers.

While detached houses first claimed a right to a name, terrace houses soon followed suit, even though they had a statutory number as well. Often a plaque was incorporated into the design of the façade so that the owner could have the house name added if they wished. Alternatives included gilded lettering on fanlights or even coloured leaded glass. Favourite early themes were royalty (Victoria, Albert, Adelaide, Alexandra); great houses (Cliveden, Chatsworth, Hardwick); place names representing favourite destinations, birthplaces or just exotic faraway lands (St Kitts, Lamorna); combinations of pleasant associations (Sunnybank, Meadowview, Rose Villa).

With the burgeoning of the suburbs naming took on a greater significance in the desire to emphasise individuality and, critically, ownership. On a practical level house names were often needed for identification until the local authority adopted the road and instigated a formal numbering. At this point the naming of houses was even extended to Hollywood stars (Barrymore), jokes (Haventwedonewell) or combined Christian names (Brymoy).

349		351	352
		353	354
350			
		355	356	357

349 Carved stone plaque on Clarence Cottage; Regent's Park, London; early 19C.

350 Suspended wooden sign over front porch (Thirlmere); Writtle, Essex; 1930s.

351 Carved stone Gothic Revival gate pier (The Tower); Hampstead, London; c. 1870.

352 Cast metal plaque on gate pier (Laburnum); Modbury, Devon; late 19C.

353 Painted glass on door light (Parliament Hill Mansions); Kentish Town, London; c. 1890.

354 Arts and Crafts gilded lettering on front door (Garden Corner); Chelsea, London; 1906.

355 Incised plaque set on wall of house (Hardwicke); Chelmsford, Essex; 1915.

356 Art Deco keystone over entrance to block of flats (Number 50); Knightsbridge, London; 1930s.

357 Screw-on DIY plastic letters on metal gate, (Kuala Lumpur); Eel Pie Island, London; 1960s.

Renderings

Rendering a building was done for a variety of reasons: weatherproofing, draughtproofing or fireproofing. It was an essential finish to a cob building as without it the walls were liable to disintegrate. Renders covered cheap or unfashionable building materials with a smooth and cohesive finish, e.g. on inferior bricks, rubblestone or a stone too hard to work to a fine finish. They were often a later addition.

Roughcast or harling (the term usually used in Scotland and Ireland) added small stones, grit, and even shells to the wet plaster mixture and then applied it to the walls, giving a softer effect than pebbledash where the dry pebbles were thrown at the wet plaster.

During the second half of the 18th century, in an attempt to make houses look as Classical as possible (and by association built of stone), there was much experimentation with covering bricks with plaster, known as stucco, in imitation of fine stone blocks. Once a successful formula was discovered it was widely used and whole terraces of houses were stuccoed giving impressively unified results. Parker's Roman Cement, patented in 1796, was the first stucco that could be relied on not to fall off in a short space of time. This was improved upon by Joseph Aspdin's Portland Cement (patented in 1824) which was stronger. Defining selected areas of brick with smooth cement, for example around windows, doorcases, porches or to form quoins and rustication, became a popular form of decoration in Victorian building.

Arts and Crafts-style builders were looking for a texture that looked honest, workmanlike and rural and thus favoured roughcast. By contrast, the Modernists of the 1930s favoured a clean, white concrete finish that looked smoothly mechanical. Pebbledash became synonymous with the ubiquitous style of suburban housing. Rendering of all types also provided a surface for colour.

358 Arts and Crafts roughcast on terrace; Letchworth Garden City, Hertfordshire; 1912.

359 Smooth cement render on Modern Movement house; Dartington, Devon; 1935.

360 Harling on Scottish Baronial wing of house; Lunga, Argyll; 18C/19C.

361 Stucco terrace; Regent's Park, London; 1825.

362 Early pebbledash with ornamental timber-framing on estate cottage; Albury, Surrey; 1850s.

363 Cement render striped with brick on terrace; Kensington, London; 1883.

364 Pebbledash on modified suburban house; Colchester, Essex; 1930s (date of alterations unknown).

365 Refurbished tower block; Deptford, London; late 1960s block, late 20C refurbishment.

Decorative plasterwork

Traditionally plaster was made from lime and sand often bulked out with hair, feathers or straw; at a later date cement was added. It was used on timber-frame buildings (sometimes covering up all timber work) and also on stone.

Although associated with interior decoration, plaster has frequently been used for the decoration of exteriors. Pargetting describes the technique of making patterns on the plaster itself and is particularly characteristic of East Anglian houses. Early examples date from the 17th century, but the designs have usually been re-worked and augmented. At their simplest they are geometric repeat patterns incised on the wet plaster with combs, sticks, stamps or even wickerwork, creating a far more interesting surface than plain plaster. More elaborate patterns were reliefs which were either moulded or worked freehand, the body of the relief design created by animal hair mixed in with the plaster.

In some cases plasterwork was used to decorate the building with fashionable motifs and to cover up and update timber-framing, in competition with stone carving or cut brick. Typically 17th-century ornamentation might include swags of fruit and flowers, columns or masks.

Decorative plasterwork was revived in the late 19th century, the white plaster creating a strong contrast to red brick. The patterns filled in gables and ran along cornices and, as in earlier examples, were a way of displaying up-to-date decoration such as Art Nouveau swirls and plant forms. Sgraffito is a technique more traditionally used in Northern and Eastern Europe, but which occasionally appears on British buildings. Two contrasting layers of plaster are laid one on top of the other, and the top layer is then scraped off, creating a two-coloured design. Pargetting was revived in the 20th century but often on cement-based plaster which produced a hard-edged, more mechanical result.

366 Plaster volutes, rustication and keystone masks; Totnes, Devon; late 17C.

367 Pargetted date in cartouche on porch; Chelsworth, Suffolk; 1689.

368 Pargetted gable; Saffron Walden, Essex; 17C on 15C house.

369 Pargetting on upper storey; Clare, Suffolk; 17C plaster on 15C house.

370 Incised decoration on oriel window; Scotney Castle, Kent; 19C restoration.

371 Pargetted diaper patterns; Saffron Walden, Essex; 17C/18C.

372 Modern plasterwork decoration in pargetted style on cottage; Writtle, Essex.

373 Plaster relief on cornice, ribbons and festoons; Hampstead, London; c. 1880.

374 Sgraffito decoration on bungalow; Birchington-on-Sea, Kent; 1882.

375 Relief plasterwork between ground- and first-floor windows; St John's Wood, London; 1890s.

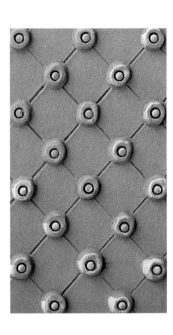

Coade stone

Coade stone was manufactured in Lambeth from 1769 until 1821. During its most successful period the company was run by Eleanor Coade and after her death by a relation, William Croggan, who then sold the business on. The moulds and models were finally bought by a sculptor, J. M. Blashfield, who had worked with the firm and who moved it to Stamford in Lincolnshire.

This patent stone provided a very extensive range of external embellishments: keystones, plaques, paterae, friezes, capitals, bas-reliefs, rusticated blocks, voussoirs, caryatids, statues, vases, urns, even garden seats (as well as non-domestic ornamentation such as figures of Britannia or Royal Coats of Arms) The great success of Coade stone stemmed from its ability to provide fashionable ornament in quantity. This was extremely useful for the builders and architects of the fast-expanding terraces and squares of London and other cities, particularly as the Building Act of 1774 put further restrictions on the use of wood on façades as a fire-prevention measure.

Coade stone was especially suitable for the delicate exterior detail applied on façades and popularised by Robert Adam during the last quarter of the 18th century. The company responded quickly to changing fashions, and produced pieces in Neo-Classical, Greek Revival and Egyptian styles. Among the most popular and typical of their details were the rusticated blocks used as quoins and keystones, and the voussoirs which emphasised the arched openings for windows and doors. These were termed vermiculated (random groovings, like a worm-cast) congelated (like icicles) or punctured (with dots and spots). Equally popular were keystones ornamented with female masks, classical gods and satyr heads, bucrania and ram's heads, which gave individuality to otherwise uniform doorways on terraces and squares.

376 Panel of guilloche pattern; Adam Street, London; c. 1770.

377 Ram's head and festoon on frieze, palmettes and egg and dart on capital of porch; Chandos House, Marylebone, London; c. 1770.

378 Panel with festoon, ribbons and paterae; Hume House, Portman Square, London; 1775.

379 Fluted fan over doorcase; Bloomsbury; London; c. 1780–90.

380 Mask keystone with vermiculated voussoirs over doorcase; Marylebone, London; late 1770s.

381 Bacchic mask keystone over doorcase; Marylebone, London; c. 1790.

382 Male herm supporting porch; Schomberg House, London; 1791.

383 Female herms on terrace; Regent's Park, London; 1820–21.

Paint

As exterior surfaces are in constant need of being recoated, paint is usually an ephemeral detail. Primarily its purpose is to protect (wood and iron have always needed paint treatments to prevent rot and rust), but paint can also ornament, decorate and express individuality.

Early lead-based paint was coloured with earth pigments: browns, greys, off-whites, dull greens, red ochre and black. During the 18th century it was recommended that gates and railings should be 'invisible' green; window sashes were often stone coloured, and front doors favoured a dark colour. Cream was the favourite colour of the late 19th century, while bright white became a 20th-century classic. Brick and stone were never intended to be painted, although roughly built stone cottages were often whitewashed for extra impermeability. Renders all lent themselves to colour washes: the traditional method was limewash, some areas becoming associated with particular shades, such as 'Suffolk pink'. Originally stucco was intended to mimic the colour of stone with the rustication emphasised by darker paintwork to give a far darker result than is expected today.

The development of fast, chemically based colours during the second half of the 19th century vastly widened the choices, and it cost no more to paint something in a bright colour than in the more traditional hues. Easy access to colour also gave people the ability to differentiate themselves from their neighbours. One author wrote in 1924 that despite the shortage of money for building materials one now had 'the sudden astonishing discovery of colour' (*The Smaller House* published by Architectural Press) which gave a house added interest at no extra cost. (He suggested primrose roughcast with jade green paintwork.) Strong exterior colours were revived in the 1960s, a period notorious for challenging historical correctness. By the end of the century authentic period colours were made commercially available by the heritage industry.

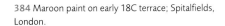

384 Maroon paint on early 18C terrace; Spitalfields, London.

385 Yellow ochre limewash on estate cottage; Badminton, Gloucestershire.

386 Pink colour-washed 15C hall house with later additions; Easthorpe, Essex.

387 Green and yellow paint on rendered cottage; Fishguard, Pembrokeshire.

388 Rendered cottage painted with *trompe-l'oeil* heavy stone blocks; Kirkmichael, Ayrshire.

389 Red-painted brick, 1950s end-of-terrace house; Stevenage New Town, Hertfordshire.

390 Red paint and black creosote on seaside summer bungalow; Southwold, Suffolk.

391 Dividing colour line on stone terrace, dated 1764 on lintel; Garlieston, Dumfries and Galloway.

392 Multi-coloured individual façades on mid-19C terrace; Kentish Town, London.

393 Blue painted early 19C terrace; Highgate, London.

Real timber-frame

The methods of building with timber-frame reveal themselves when looking at the exteriors of houses and cottages. It was a slow development from primitive hut building to the creation of substantial dwellings. The fundamental problem was to create a walled, roofed space without filling the interior with supports (aisle posts) and beams.

One of the earliest was construction with 'cruck' beams. Single, curved pieces of wood were split in two and then erected — like wishbones — to be held fast by a ridge beam that created a roof ridge and held the structure securely. Once this was achieved the infilling of the bay (space between the upright beams) could be done from wattle and daub, made from whatever was locally available. The limitation of this system lay in its dependence on the availability of lengths of curved timber, and the difficulty in obtaining any height.

Regional differences are marked but the two basic construction types are generally known as post-and-truss and box-frame. Both involved setting the beams at right angles with the roof supported by purlins (beams running from roof ridge to eave) and tie beams (which created the base of the triangle, holding the roof rigid). King posts and crown posts linked the tie beam to the roof ridge or purlins. These methods allowed space for a proper upper floor and for the creation of jetties. While the jetty has practical uses, it can also be grand and decorative and it has always been the most imitated — and impressive — feature in the vocabulary of timber-framing.

The arrangement of beams may have been driven by their function, but the effects were also decorative and by the late 16th century, particularly in the Shropshire area, there were ostentatious displays of timber patterns that bore no relation to load-bearing requirements.

394 Cruck frame on medieval cottage; Osmaston, Derbyshire.

395 Small-panel framing on manor house; Lower Brockhampton House, Worcestershire; 14C.

396 Close-studded timber-framing with jettied gable end; Manuden, Essex.

397 Detail of pegged joints; Manuden, Essex.

398 Timber-bracing around windows, limed wood and limewashed plaster; Lavenham, Suffolk.

399 Carved beam; Paycocke's, Coggeshall, Essex; c. 1500.

400 Jettied timber-frame houses; Lavenham, Suffolk.

401 Close-studded façade; Stoke-by-Nayland, Suffolk.

402 Brick nogging below jetty; Colchester, Essex; 16C.

403 Close-panelling with ornamental infilling; Ludlow, Shropshire; 1619.

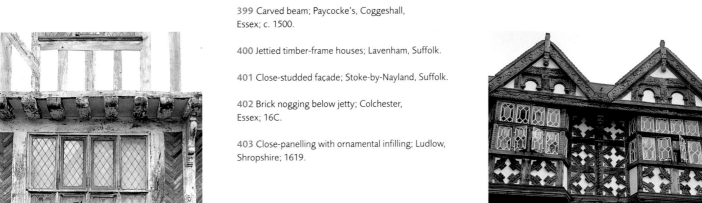

Timber-frame as ornament

While bargeboards were a key element in giving a house or cottage a picturesque look in the early 19th century, half-timbering or timber-framing (with which bargeboards are originally associated) was assimilated until a little later. Decorative timber-frame, often used in conjunction with render, was a popular choice for estate cottages and model villages.

It was also one of the features picked out from the vernacular vocabulary by the architects of the Arts and Crafts movement, for example, Richard Norman Shaw who created gables and jetties patterned with timbers on his large country houses. Some Arts and Crafts houses, as can be expected, had genuine structural timber-frames. M. Hugh Baillie Scott built such a cottage at Findon 'because it seemed peculiarly adapted to a district where its cost was no greater than a nine-inch brick wall'.

The Edwardians showed a great sentimentality towards the countryside: publishers, illustrators and postcard manufacturers produced numerous images of traditional country cottages, a large proportion of which were half-timbered. Some derelict old cottages were pillaged for beams that were incorporated into new houses, and the fashion for emphasising beams with black paint dates from this period. For the speculative builder in the suburbs, a slice of romantic country life could be suggested with the application of beam patterns on the exterior, even if it was on a block of flats with nine floors. Thus the much-derided Mock-Tudor style was born.

By the end of the 20th century houses were still being decorated with applied wood 'half-timbered' gables, presumably because this detail had become deeply embedded in the nation's psyche as a symbol of home.

404			408	409	410
				412	
405			411		
	406	407		413	

404 Timber-frame ornament on turrets and gables, cream paint and pebbledash; Waddesdon, Buckinghamshire; c. 1880s.

405 Double cottage with timber-frame, tile-hanging, stone and brick; Ticehurst, Kent; mid-19C.

406 Double cottage painted with timber-framing patterns; Bridgenorth, Shropshire; late 19C.

407 Black-and-white timber-frame decoration at roof level; Grim's Dyke, Harrow, London; 1872.

408 Block of flats; Maida Vale, London; 1930s.

409 End-of-terrace house in half timber with jetty and fake pegged joints; Port Sunlight, Cheshire; c. 1900.

410 Diamond-pane windows and timber-framing on housing development; Maldon, Essex; 2000.

411 Mock Tudor flats; Highgate, London; c. 1928–30.

412 Cottage with wavy-edge beams; Kingswood, Surrey; early 20C.

413 Suburban house with matching garage, diamond-leaded casement windows; Epsom, Surrey; 1930s.

Ceramics

Until the invention of a frost-proof tile there was little opportunity to use ceramic tiles as exterior decoration, and until they were mass-produced there could be little demand. During the Gothic Revival period, however, there was a renewed interest in medieval flooring tiles (inlaid with patterns of contrasting coloured clays) and the encaustic tile, which was frost-proof, was developed during the 1830s.

The potter, Herbert Minton, was the prime mover in the re-introduction of tiling. Experimenting with techniques as early as 1828, he bought a share in Samuel Wright's patent for mechanical tile production in 1830. Minton also worked closely with the Gothic Revival architect A. W. Pugin (who enthusiastically advocated a public statue of Minton holding up a tile), and commercial production got underway. Thinner glazed wall tiles went into production around 1840. Encaustic tiles were popular for paths and doorsteps and occasionally as a decorative frieze on façades around doors or windows. The earliest colours were white and red; by the 1880s buff, brown, black, blue, green and pink had extended the range.

Small, geometrically shaped tiles and tesserae for mosaics were made to accompany the encaustic tiles and widen the scope of their applications. Hygiene was a buzzword of the late 19th century and thus glazed tile porches became extremely popular, being both easy to clean and highly decorative. Many applications of ceramic decoration were commercial, rather than domestic, although occasional examples appear, such as the work done by the sculptor Gilbert Bayes for the St Pancras Housing Association in majolica (tin-glazed earthenware), which enjoyed a revival at the turn of the century. Panels of cladding which produced colour and texture were typical on new building of the 1950s, and tiling was often introduced at this date.

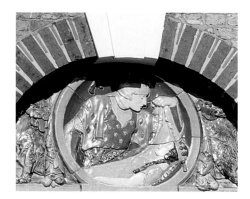

| 414 | | | 418 | 419 | 420 |
| 415 | 416 | 417 | 421 | | 422 |

414 Encaustic tiles on front path, steps and porch; Clapham, London; house 1850s, (tiling later).

415 Encaustic tile panel set above front door; Hornsey,, London; 1870s.

416 Mosaic doorstep incorporating number of house; Camden, London; 1870s.

417 Majolica tympanum to window (depicting Sleeping Beauty) in St Pancras Housing Association flats; Camden; 1938.

418 Tiled porch incorporating dado; Cardiff; c. 1900.

419 Art Nouveau glazed tiled porch; Bath; c. 1900.

420 Majolica finial on communal washing posts at St Pancras Housing Association flats; Camden, London; 1938.

421 Random coloured tiles as decorative cladding on local authority flats; Camden, London; 1950s.

422 Glazed brick wall of flats; Bermondsey, London; 1990s.

Cladding

Tile-hanging (also known as weather-tiling), slate-hanging and weatherboarding or clapboard were all originally used to protect timber-framed, brick or stone walls from the extremes of the British climate. Frequently, the upper storey only was clad with the overlapping tiles, slates or boards which tilted out at the base to deflect water away from the wall. These solutions were regional and the earliest examples probably date from the 17th century. Tile-hanging and weatherboarding are both particularly characteristic of, although not exclusive to, south-east England whereas slate-hanging is mainly found in Devon and Cornwall.

Tiles designed to imitate brick, known as mathematical tiles, were an invention of the Georgian period and used to clad houses. Initially this was probably a way of updating an earlier house by disguising a timber-frame or altered window patterns. After the onset of the 1784 brick tax, they were also used on new buildings.

In many cases cladding was added as an improvement and tended to date from the later Georgian period. It was also, however, an opportunity for gentle ornamentation, as decoratively shaped tiles created interesting effects of light and shade and contrasting coloured slate and clay tiles further enriched the patterning. J. C. Loudon wrote in his *Encyclopedia of Cottage, Farm and Villa Architecture* (1833) that tile-hanging gave a 'homely and comfortable appearance'. Tile-hanging made the transition to the ordinary early 20th-century house with its token section applied to gable or bay, but once the tiles were machine-made they lost their wobbly charm. Weatherboarding fared better and 'waney-edged' (edges untrimmed) elm boards were a popular feature in the early part of the century.

Architecture of the 1950s and 1960s made much use of contrasting sections of cladding, as prefabricated panels and new materials such as plastics increased the options of colour and texture. Cladding with thin metal sheeting was a late 20th-century direction.

| 423 | 424 | | 427 | 428 | 429 |
| 425 | 426 | | 430 | 431 | 432 |

423 Black mathematical tiles applied onto brick terrace; Brighton, Sussex; terrace 1798–1807, tiles applied later.

424 Tile-hung upper storey on cottage; Petworth, Sussex.

425 Tile hanging and weatherboarding on estate cottages; Groombridge, Kent.

426 Tile hanging as decorative section above window; Reading, Berkshire; c. 1870.

427 Cladding with cement tiles, Span housing development; Blackheath, London; 1950s.

428 Slate-hung house; St Ives, Cornwall; 18C.

429 Decorative slate-hanging in two colours, living accommodation above shop; Dartmouth, Devon; c. 1880.

430 Weatherboarded cottage; Roxwell, Essex.

431 Pre-cast concrete 'weatherboard' on public housing; Writtle, Essex; 1950s.

432 Timber cladding on upper storey of rebuilt mews; Highbury, London; 1990s.

Brick

For centuries Britain lagged behind continental Europe in brick-making, and until the 15th century there are only incidental examples of their use. Techniques of brick-making and brick-laying came from Flanders, Holland and Northern Germany (where there was no stone for building) via close trading links with towns in Eastern England. In 1571 Elizabeth I granted a charter to the Tylers' and Bricklayers' Company, an indication that brick was fast becoming an important building material not only for new buildings but also as a fireproof solution for 'a multitude of chimneys lately erected', as reported by William Harrison in his *Description of England* (1577). Bricks could also strengthen existing timber-frame houses, by replacing the wattle and daub with nogging. The advantages were clear: bricks could usually be made near the site (suitable clay was to be found in much of the country; the clay was dug in autumn and made into bricks in spring); since they were made in moulds bricks came in a variety of convenient sizes, and they were resilient and warmer than stone.

From the outset the decorative possibilities of bricks were fully exploited, as they could be laid in patterns of contrasting colours and combined with other materials such as flint and stone. Bricks were laid in varying 'bonds' or combinations of stretchers (the brick's longest side) with headers (its shortest). The most common was English bond which alternated courses of stretchers and headers. Flemish bond, which became the most popular in the 18th century, alternated stretchers and headers within every course. Stretching bond, since it only used stretchers, made the most economical use of bricks. A labour-intensive technique called tuck pointing (defining the mortar with a thin white line) demonstrated conspicuous expenditure on a façade.

Bricks could be cut or painstakingly rubbed with a piece of grit-stone to make decorative cornices, pilasters, window and door frames. Special soft, smooth red bricks were produced for this gauged brickwork and laid to fit tightly so that the mortar was hardly visible. These techniques were highly prized in the 17th century and revived when exposed brickwork was reappraised in the 1850s after decades of stucco.

Originally bricks came in a variety of colours depending on clay and firing, so when brick-making became mechanised at the end of the 19th century the subtle variations of handmade bricks were lost. Fashions in colour also changed. From the late 17th century to the 1730s the style was for red or purple and dark grey with red dressings. Later, browner, greyer more stone-like colours were preferred, which in turn gave way to yellow and cream during the Regency period.

A brick tax that lasted from 1784 until 1850 meant that double duty was levied on large or ornamental bricks. As soon as the tax was repealed Victorian brick-makers produced a wider range of colours and shapes, pressed with patterns and motifs. The production of cheap bricks was made possible in the late 1870s when a seam of clay with a high carbon content was discovered at Fletton

near Peterborough that could be pressed straight into moulds and put through a kiln that burnt continuously. So-called Fletton bricks thus became a by-word for economy. Inspiration for polychrome brickwork came in part from illustrations of Venetian Gothic buildings in John Ruskin's *Stones of Venice* (1851–53). The author later commented: 'I have had an indirect influence on nearly every cheap villa builder between this and Bromley'.

Dark red bricks returned to favour in the 1870s to 1890s only to be condemned in 1906 as a 'scarlet fever' by the Arts and Crafts architect M. Hugh Baillie Scott. With mass production bricks became totally predictable in size, colour and texture. Subsequently, and often in response to the conservation lobby, many companies started to manufacture bricks in a variety of different textures and motley colourings.

433 Brick cottage; Maldon, Essex; 18C.

434 Estate cottage with decorative brick and timber-framing; Albury, Surrey; 1850s.

435 Red stretchers and blue headers laid in Flemish bond with red gauged brick over window and door; Overton, Hampshire; late 18C/early 19C.

436 Detail of striped red brick and black-glazed brick on semi-detached cottage; Mudford, Somerset; 1860.

437 Red machine brick on suburban house; Cardiff; 1920s.

Brick

438 Brick nogging within timber-framing; Aldeburgh, Suffolk; 16C.

439 Brick side wall, showing stucco quoins of façade; Sutton House, Hackney, London; 16C.

440 Diamond-patterned brick on almshouse; Farnham, Surrey; 1619.

441 Cut-brick window surround; Cromwell House, Highgate, London; 1637–40.

442 Brick laid in English bond, Norfolk, 17C.

443 Tuck pointed brick laid in Flemish bond; Marylebone, London; 18C.

444 Brick bow in red and vitreous brick; Benson, Oxfordshire; late 18C.

438	439	440		445	446	447
441	442			448	449	
443	444			450	451	

445 Brickwork showing lime mortar; Orford, Suffolk; 18C.

446 Gault brick; Bury St Edmunds, Suffolk; early 19C.

447 Cream bricks in stretcher bond; Kentish Town, London; 1992.

448 Polychrome brickwork in grey, red and white on terrace; Reading, Berkshire; late 19C.

449 Cut and rubbed brick pediment over porch with Renaissance Revival motifs; Hampstead, London; 1890s.

450 Grey brick walls with red brick quoins, string course and window surrounds; Sulhamstead, Berkshire; 1906–1912.

451 Mottled bricks, public housing; Bristol; 1960s.

Brick houses

452 Gate tower; Sissinghurst, Kent; 1560s.

453 Classical house with brickwork quoins; Balls Park, Hertford, Hertfordshire; 1643.

454 Terrace; Bridgewater, Somerset; 1720s.

455 Terrace; Islington, London; late 18C.

456 Terrace; Liverpool, Merseyside; late 18C.

		454		457	458	459
452	453				460	461
455	456				462	463

457 Terrace of gault brick and flint; Sudbury, Suffolk; early 19C.

458 Polychrome brick cottage; Orford, Suffolk; mid-19C.

459 Brick almshouses, Nantwich, Cheshire; mid-19C.

460 Stone with pale brick; Great Torrington, Devon; 1880s.

461 Terrace of brick with terracotta Gothic decorations; Port Sunlight, Cheshire; 1896.

462 Brickwork emphasised with white mortar; Hampstead, London; 1930s.

463 Mottled brick house with waney-edged weatherboard gable; Chelmsford, Essex; 1950s.

Terracotta

An alternative to cutting and rubbing brick to provide decorative embellishments was to make sections of ornamental terracotta. Clay was fired in patterned moulds to produce a material which was denser and harder than brick, but of the same basic natural material which thus combined well with it.

A few grand Tudor houses, such as Sutton Place and Layer Marney, had terracotta detail on, for example, window frames and parapets (possibly made by Italian craftsmen), but it was never widely used during this period. In the 18th century a stone-coloured version of terracotta was marketed by Eleanor Coade (*see* Coade stone).

When stucco fell from fashion in the 1860s an interest in terracotta re-emerged, together with all types of ornamental brickwork and general polychrome effects. Terracotta was mainly manufactured in deep red, buff (popular in the 1880s) or a greyish white. Essentially used in urban situations as its smooth surface repelled soot to some extent, terracotta was also cheaper and lighter than ornamental stone (the blocks of terracotta were cast hollow and then filled with concrete when in place). However, terracotta could warp in firing and was therefore unreliable for use on large sections such as window frames and door surrounds. Among the leading producers were Doulton, Blashfield's of Stamford (who took over the remains of the Coade business) and Edwards' of Ruabon.

Characteristic terracotta details were plaques with Aesthetic Movement sunflowers, pots of lilies, Renaissance Revival swags and festoons or fashionable *japonaiseries*, such as oriental-style frets. It was also used for ornamental roof finials and chimney pots, particularly those moulded with Elizabethan revival or Old English patterns, such as barley-sugar twists or fleurs de lys. It was also well suited to impressive name plaques and datestones for blocks of mansion flats or workers' dwellings.

464 Terracotta cresting on gatehouse, ornamented with dolphins, egg-and-dart and guilloche patterns; Layer Marney, Essex; c. 1520.

465 Terracotta quoins and black-and-red diaper brickwork; Sutton Place, Surrey; late 16C.

466 Portrait medallion and plant-ornamented window arch on terrace; Maida Vale, London; c. 1850s–60s.

464

465

466

467   469

468

470

471   472

467 Gothic Revival leaf quatrefoil over window; Whitby, Yorkshire; c. 1860.

468 Balcony, window surrounds and cornice ornament in two-colour terracotta; Mayfair, London; c. 1890s.

469 Datestone and potted sunflower; Hampstead, London; 1874.

470 Door jamb, guilloche pattern and scrolling foliage; Knightsbridge, London; 1891.

471 Cornice blocks with festoons and winged mask; Hampstead, London; c. 1890.

472 Cornice sections with gadroon pattern and key pattern on artist's studio; St John's Wood, London; late 19C.

Iron

There is little iron ore in Britain. Shortage of wood in the 17th century (which also affected glass-making) hampered iron production as copious amounts of charcoal were needed to smelt and forge it, and early attempts to use sea-coal were not very successful. Iron was either wrought, by being hammered into shape or cast in a primitive manner by running the pig-iron (iron too brittle to be wrought) into sand moulds. Early use of iron in buildings was thus restricted to the essential: nails, hinges, and structural rods.

In the 17th century, the arrival in Britain of skilled Huguenot metalworkers such as Jean Tijou demonstrated the potential for decorative ironwork. His wrought-iron gates, screens and balconies in richly curving exuberant three-dimensional patterns was published in 1693 in *A New Booke of Drawings Invented and Desined by John Tijou*. This became a pattern-book for smiths during much of the 18th century. Cast iron became a viable and cheaper alternative once Abraham Darby had simplified the smelting process by substituting charcoal with coke which burnt at a hotter temperature. Isaac Ware pointed out in 1756 that cast iron was 'very serviceable to the builder and a vast expense is saved in many cases by using it (for) rails and balusters it makes a rich and massy appearance when it has cost very little, and wrought iron, much less substantial, would cost a vast sum'.

The cast-iron industry expanded hugely between 1750 and 1820. Foundries were started up strategically close to coal fields and to ports (which imported pig iron) notably Abraham Darby's Coalbrookdale in Shropshire, Wilkinson's in Staffordshire and the Carron Works near Falkirk in Scotland, which produced quantities of railings, gates, fanlights, balconies, window guards, exterior lamps and overthrows — the perfect ornament for the vastly growing number of terraces and villas and an excellent foil to the equally popular stucco. The repertoire of patterns expanded rapidly, many of them becoming standard for decades. A pattern book, first published in 1823 by L. N. Cottingham as *The Ornamental Metalworker's Director*, included pieces in what he termed Grecian, Roman and Gothic styles. Verandas, porches and window canopies were popular early 19th-century additions.

Strictly utilitarian fittings made in cast iron included guttering and down-pipes, ventilation gratings and coal plates (removable covers set into the pavement, enabling coal to be tipped directly into the coal cellar). Cast-iron windows were principally used for warehouses, chapels and schools but were an economic option in the 1820s and 1850s for cottages and almshouses with decorative glazing.

By the Victorian period, cast-iron ornament was becoming far heavier, and linear patterns were giving way to bulky balusters, elaborate scrollwork and dense foliage. Following Pugin's view that construction should not be concealed but 'avowed', door hinges, locks and nails were celebrated in

473 Iron balconies, balcony brackets, window guards and railings, stucco terrace; Brighton, Sussex; c.1815–20.

474 Gothic Revival iron door furniture on stone terrace; Castle Cary, Somerset; 1876.

475 Art Deco ironwork on glass entrance door and balconies on blocks of flats; Holborn, London; 1930s.

476 Cast-iron coal plate set in pavement covering shute into coal cellar; Holborn, London; 19C.

the manner of medieval smiths and rendered as 'rich and beautiful decorations'. The Gothic Revival changed the emphasis of ironwork as an exterior feature, as elaborate door ironwork, finials, pennant weathervanes and roof cresting were added to the repertoire of ornaments available to the builder.

The value of cast iron lay in the way it could take ornament, but it was heavy and brittle and, by the end of the 19th century, unfashionable. Repetitive cast ironwork was anathema to adherents of the Arts and Crafts style who wanted metalwork to have a hand-wrought, hammered look. Subsequent manufacturing developments in the iron and steel industry resulted in metal being produced in a wide range of component parts. These became the basis for metalwork on gates, balconies, doors, and finish became more important than ornament. The late 20th-century use of metalwork divided into two streams: the craft-based, and one which explored the use of industrial materials.

Iron

477 Wrought-iron entrance gates on stone piers; Frampton-on-Severn, Gloucestershire; 18C.

478 Overthrow and railings; Wells, Somerset; mid-18C.

479 Iron window fixture on casement window; Montacute, Somerset.

480 Railings and drainpipe; Burford, Oxfordshire; 19C.

481 Ironwork bootscraper and niche ornament; Bloomsbury, London; 1770s.

| 477 | 478 | | 482 | 483 | 484 | 485 |
| 479 | 480 | 481 | 486 | | 487 | 488 |

482 Ironwork and its shadow on veranda; Wells, Somerset; early 19C.

483 Cresting on garden wall; Saffron Walden, Essex; 19C.

484 Section of continuous iron balcony with Vitruvian scroll on terrace; Belgravia, London; c. 1830 (balcony design 1780s).

485 Gate pier and railings; Notting Hill Gate, London; mid-19C.

486 Exterior lamp and railings on flats; Kensington, London; 1901.

487 Balcony over porch; Hampstead Garden Suburb, London; 1930s.

488 Garden gate; Dean Village, Edinburgh; 1990s' gate 19C railings.

Corrugated iron

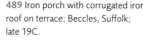

489 Iron porch with corrugated iron roof on terrace; Beccles, Suffolk; late 19C.

490 Corrugated iron porch roof and cottage roof; Mudford, Somerset.

491 Corrugated iron porch with slate roof; Plockton, Highlands.

The invention in the late 1820s of corrugated iron is credited to the founder of the Institute of Engineers, Henry Robinson. It was immediately recognised as invaluable for building large roof spans, and therefore particularly useful in the construction of barns and warehouses. One of the first people to write about it was J. C. Loudon in his *Encyclopaedia of Cottage, Farm and Villa Architecture* (1833), recommending its use in door panels, cottage roofs and 'portable houses'. Loudon pointed out that its durability depended on the application of oil or tar paints, and that iron cottages should be covered in evergreen creeper 'to moderate the effect of changes in the exterior temperature'.

Corrugated iron was light and easily transported by rail (or by ship to distant colonies), and manufacturers such as Boulton and Paul of Norwich and William Cooper of the Old Kent Road in London responded by producing large ranges of 'portable' or prefabricated houses, cottages and bungalows as well as cricket pavilions, churches, billiard rooms, village halls and mission rooms. The relative cheapness of corrugated iron buildings (only a brick foundation was required) meant that they were popular for holiday and seaside homes, fishing and hunting lodges. They also provided low-cost housing for gardeners, gamekeepers and estate workers, which was useful in remote places where the transport of traditional building materials was problematic.

Cooper's turn-of-the-century catalogue describes the material used in its houses as being 'standard Birmingham gauge only, truly and evenly corrugated, thickly coated with pure Silesian spelter'. Cooper's also supplied ornamental iron pinnacles and roof cresting in 'approved Gothic designs'. However, in many areas, restrictive by-laws prevented the proliferation of such buildings.

489   490

492   494
        493
495

491

496   497

492 Corrugated iron replacing stone or thatch as roof; Dinton, Wiltshire.

493 House with double-storey wooden balcony; Medstead, Hampshire; late 19C/early 20C.

494 Holiday cottage with wooden balcony; Aberdaron, Gwynedd; early 20C.

495 Bungalow with wooden bargeboards and iron roof cresting; Amberley, Gloucestershire; early 20C.

496 Bungalow with brick chimneys and bay window; Boughton, Kent; late 19C/early 20C.

497 Corrugated iron roof, public housing; Queen Camel, Somerset; c. 1925.

Paths and drives

In a front garden of any size there is a need for a clear path to the front door, and in many cases a historic alternative route to the back door or tradesman's entrance. The pattern is usually set by the style of architecture: thus the formal, four-square house, designed with a central doorway, would have a straight path leading directly up to it. However, as soon as a house had an asymmetrical façade, the path could be correspondingly serpentine. The planting of the garden frequently emphasised these features. Equally the status of the house could be immediately apparent from the existence of a carriage drive — a feature subsequently adapted for the car. While the detached garage was a clear successor to the coach house, the notion of the integral garage which appeared in the second decade of the 20th century led to a revised planning of paths and entrances.

Until skirts ceased to sweep the ground, the laying of terraces, cobbles and gravel walks was an important consideration; unmetalled roads and horse-traffic contributed to an unpleasant muddiness that had to be avoided. Tiled paths were a perfect urban solution as they met the criteria of being both ornamental and practical. Crazy paving, like rockeries and cinder walling, was also typical of the early 20th century, and characteristic of a period that sought to create good effects out of waste products. Later, clean, modern, minimalist effects were created with materials such as bonded gravel, slate and large pebbles. The noise made from walking on pebbles was considered an added security factor.

The advent of ready-mixed concrete and tarmacadam led to the creation of many gloomy paths and drives, and perhaps contributed to the nostalgia for the timeless vision of the flower-bordered cottage path.

498 Stone paving to stone terrace; New Town, Edinburgh; early 19C.

499 Brick house with brick path; Stedham, Sussex; early 18C house, modern path.

500 Cottage garden path; Little Missenden, Buckinghamshire.

501 Curving path of encaustic tile on terrace; Cardiff; 1920s.

502 Slate path and loose pebbles; Chelsea, London; 1990s.

503 Hedge with clipped castellations bordering concrete path; Aston Rowant, Oxfordshire.

504 Entrance with pond, steps and ramp; Blackheath, London; 1968.

505 Drive to garage and side path to house; Sutton, Surrey; 1920s.

506 Curved sweep for car to front of house; Putney, London; 1930s.

Boundaries

The house-dweller can immediately engender a sense of security by encircling the plot to create a defensible space, and this boundary is often the detail which best expresses how the inhabitant wishes to be viewed by the outside world. A 14th-century cottage in Chaucer's *Nun's Priest's Tale* was 'enclosed all about with stikkes, and a drye dych without', suggesting that the desire to fortify even insignificant houses has a long history.

The gatehouse or lodge is an extension of this desire in its implication that someone is permanently guarding the entrance. For the most part, however, people have had to content themselves with a gate and a wall, fence or hedge. For aristocrats, carved stone heraldic crests perched on gate piers symbolised a watchful presence, for others a range of balls, cones, urns, eagles and pineapples (signifying hospitality and welcome) were used. In 1756 Isaac Ware wrote that a niche was an essential part of a gate pier in order to provide a seat for the weary visitor arriving by foot 'to take in refreshment and the prospect'. In the 18th century the grandest gates were usually of wrought iron, and even terrace houses sometimes emphasised their entrances with iron overthrows (arches which usually incorporated a lamp). In the interests of uniformity, gates and railings were supplied by the builder along the length of the terrace, while individual choice was restricted to detached houses.

By the end of the 19th century there was a revival of interest in hedges, wooden gates and picket fences. For example hedges were specified for Hampstead Garden Suburb as a deliberate move against urban iron or cheap walling made from clinker. A late 20th-century enthusiasm for the almost total privacy afforded by fast-growing cypress leylandii trees led to demands for a law limiting the height of hedge boundaries.

507 Limestone slab fence; Filkins, Oxfordshire.

508 Granite wall with white quartz boulders along top; Newport, Pembrokeshire.

509 Unpainted wooden picket fence; Crofton, Wiltshire.

510 Topiary hedge and bank; East Lambrook, Somerset.

507		511	513
			512
508		514	
509	510	515	516

511 Iron railings; Dedham, Essex; late 19C.

512 Arts and Crafts wooden fencing and gates; Bedford Park, London; 1880s.

513 Cinder wall, wooden lap fence and hedge on terrace housing; Highgate, London; c. 1900.

514 Solid iron fencing and gate piers; Clifton, Bristol; c. 1850.

515 Post and chain; Burnham Market, Norfolk.

516 Random wall made from scrap and rubble; Frinton-on-Sea, Essex.

Gates

517 Gate piers with eagles and niches; Mapperton, Dorset; 17C.

518 Gateway into wall surmounted by carved stone fragments on former vicarage; Burford, Oxfordshire; 18C.

519 Stone gateway carved with house name and owners' monogram; Bath; c. 1870s.

520 Yew topiary gate piers in traditional shape; East Bergholt, Suffolk.

521 Cast-iron pedestrian gate at bottom of carriage drive; Coalbrookdale, Shropshire; mid-19C.

522 Cast-iron Gothic Revival gateway with stone gate lodge; Kirkmichael, Ayrshire; mid-19C.

523 Aesthetic Movement gates and railings, decorated with sunflowers and japonaiserie fans; Castle Cary, Somerset; 1880s.

524 Boarded garden gate in farm wall; Marlborough, Devon.

525 Home-made gate decorated with ship's half model; Whitby, Yorkshire; early 20C.

526 Wooden gates in garden wall; Charlton Mackrell, Somerset; early 20C.

527 White picket fence and beech arch; Walthamstow, Essex.

528 Galvanised iron grille gate and fence combined with willow-wattle fencing; Islington, London; 2001.

Glossary of House Types

529 Brick almshouses (Abbot's Hospital); Guildford, Surrey; 1619–22.

530 Almshouses; Bitton, Gloucestershire; 1830–40.

Almshouse

Housing for the poor and needy, supported by donation of alms (money or land). The earliest existing foundation is the Hospital of St Cross in Winchester, founded for 13 poor men in 1136. Early foundations were principally connected to the church and monarchy, but the pre-Reformation belief that a failure to be charitable meant a spell in purgatory led to many almshouses being established from the late 15C by increasingly wealthy landowners and merchants. The design of alms-houses tended to follow prevailing style. In plan they were frequently a collegiate quadrangle incorporating a chapel and communal hall, although small endowments often funded just a single row of cottages. They were frequently single-storey. The simplicity of the accommodation was sometimes at odds with the elaborate heraldic display that clearly indicated the source of the endowment. The establishment of almshouses continued after the Reformation. Increasingly found-ations were created by town guilds and corporations rather than individuals. The style tended to restrained Classicism and figures of Charity, Faith and Hope replaced founders' statues. Styles for 19C almshouses were generally Eliza-bethan or Gothic Revival. 53, 81, 440, 529, 530

Back-to-back housing

Forms of Victorian working-class terrace*, built to a very high density, predominantly in the industrial north. There were many regional variations which made maximum use of land: in some the houses were literally back-to-back, opening out either side onto a court, row, alley or road; in others the rows faced each other across small yards. Back-to-back housing along with cellar dwellings and narrow streets were condemned as unhealthy by the Public Health Act of 1875; this and local by-laws prevented further building.

Bastle house

Particular to the Scottish–English borders, built during the Border Wars (c. 1300–1707), this two-storey house provided a retreat for both livestock and people. Animals were corralled at ground level and the people lived on the upper floor which was reached by an exterior stone staircase. See also pele tower*.

Black house

Scottish single-storey double-walled house with central open hearth, typical of the Western Isles. So-called because the chimneyless interior soon became blackened with soot. Also associated with crofts*.

Block dwelling

These multi-storey blocks housing many families either in single rooms or series of rooms (flats*), were seen by housing reformers in the mid-19C as a solution allowing the workforce to live close to their employment on a small parcel of expensive land. Building techniques taken from industry and commerce were adapted to domestic use: cast-iron structures for balconies, external staircases, large roof-spans, and fireproofing techniques. The arrangement of the blocks allowed for minimal intervening space resulting in cramped conditions that were criticised by the subsequent generation of reformers. Since economy was the driving force behind the creation of these buildings there was rarely any ornament or decoration beyond some poly-chrome brickwork, and often an elaborate cartouche dating and naming the building. 31, 211, 213, 215, 238, 308, 312, 316, 317, 356, 365, 475, 531

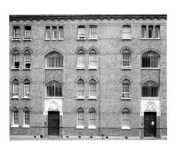

531 Brewer's Building, polychrome brick; Islington, London; 1880s.

532 Hambleton Hall built for hunting; Hambleton, Rutland; 1881.

533 Double bothy, each with single room; Kirkudbright, Dumfries and Galloway; mid-19C.

534 Bungalow with upper room and veranda; Yarmouth, Isle of Wight; 1897.

535 Timber bungalow; Wellington, Herefordshire; 1920s/1930s.

536 'The Haven' Plotland bungalow; Dunton Heath, Basildon, Essex; 1930s.

Bothy

Eighteenth-century Scottish term for a very simple, probably single-room cottage* in which unmarried estate-workers were lodged. Its original purpose fallen into disuse, the word has been used to describe a simple rustic retreat. 533

Box

A small house in the country, intended for country pursuits, often described as a hunting box or a shooting box (though not a fishing box, as fishing usually happened from a lodge*). 532

Bungalow

A westernised version of an Indian term for a simple native hut, appropriated to describe the low, sprawling housing developed by the Empire-builders of the British Raj, 'bungalow' came into general use in the 1880s. The first true British bungalow was built on the Kent coast at Birchington in 1869 as a holiday house. The siting of early bungalows was important. P. T. Harrison wrote in *Bungalow Residences* (1909) that they should be erected 'for the most part at the seaside or in the country in positions chosen for the quality of the air or for recreative facilities or other attractions'. A few architects con-

sidered bungalows worthy of attention, most famously Robert Briggs, who published *Bungalow and Country Residences* in 1891. Some of his bungalows were fairly substantial, two-storey buildings although still bungalows in spirit: 'What we mean by a bungalow is an artistic little dwelling, cheaply but soundly built with a proper regard to sanitation, and popped down in some pretty little spot with just enough accommodation for our particular needs'. The 'artistic' dwelling was also perceived as bohemian. H. G. Wells's novel *In the Days of the Comet* (1906) describes a bungalow village inhabited by 'artistic-minded and carelessly living people' occupying railway carriages turned into 'habitable little cabins for the summer holiday...improvised homes, gaily painted and with broad verandas and supplementary lean-to's'. Many such bungalows were intended only for summer use and made use of land unsuitable for permanent development on shores and riverbanks and avoided building regulations. Communities of bunga-lows grew up in areas that could be reached easily by train and bus. Typical were the so-called 'Plotlands' in Essex and Kent where east-enders from London built small rural retreats.

After the First World War bungalows lost their association with free and easy living, becoming merely a cheap housing solution. By 1928 the architect Clough Williams-Ellis described 'bungaloid growth' as 'England's most disfiguring disease'. Such developments became the catalyst for planning restrictions. 374, 390, 495, 496, 534, 535, 536

Castle

Elements of defensible medieval military buildings occasionally appeared on domestic houses (sometimes named 'castle'). Common features were castellations, battlements, arched windows, and fake arrow-loops. This form was particularly popular in Scotland for large country houses* and was also used for gatehouses* and lodges*, emphasising the defensible private space. 537

Chalet

Housing with a long sloping roof, derived from Alpine architecture. A minor British enthusiasm for Swiss style during the first half of the 19C resulted in the building of various Swiss cottages* and chalets from patterns supplied by P. F. Robinson's *Rural Architecture, or a series of designs for Ornamental Cottages*

(1823). In the 1920s and 1930s the term was commonly used to describe bungalows* where an extra bedroom was squeezed in the roof-space, or suburban housing with the chalet-roof shape. It was subsequently associated with small, insubstantial holiday-camp buildings.

Chambers

Sets of rooms providing lodgings for single men, a term particularly used for lawyers' rooms at the London Inns of Court. Albany in Piccadilly was an early purpose-built set of chambers, a conversion* in 1802 by the architect Henry Holland from a house originally built in 1770 for Lord Melbourne. 539

Chantry

Lodging for those who were paid to pray in chantry chapels (as a general rule the poor seeking food and shelter). Chantry chapels were built during the Middle Ages to offer up continuous prayers for the soul of the benefactor. When their credibility as a useful path to heaven waned, chantry chapels became obsolete and any survivors were generally used as a vicarage*. As a house name 'The Chantry' was occasionally used in the 19C for country houses in a Gothic or Elizabethan Revival style.

537 'Speedwell Castle', house built in the Gothick style; Brewood, Staffordshire; 1750.

538 Martello tower converted into Indian-style house; Paignton, Devon; 1853 (conversion).

539 Lawyers chambers; Temple, London; late 17C/early 18C.

540 Train carriage extended into bungalow; Selsey, Sussex; c. 1936.

541 Windmill conversion; Reedham, Norfolk; 1960s.

Conversion

The conversion of structures into housing is usually driven by a combination of factors: redundancy of building type, shortage of housing and desirability of the site. The value of stone building meant that substantial stone farm buildings were sometimes converted into cottages*, as at Arlington Row in Bibury, Gloucestershire in the 17C. Conversely railway carriages, insubstantial and easily transported, were converted into bungalows* during the 1920s and 1930s and placed in holiday locations. Windmills and oast houses were frequently converted during the same period. Acute housing shortages after the Second World War made the conversion of otherwise redundant buildings such as coach houses and mews* both feasible and desirable. Diminishing congregations led the Church of England to declare churches redundant from 1969 onwards and the first church to be turned into a house was finished in 1972. 538, 540, 541

Cottage

A small dwelling for someone working on the land. Most early cottages were primitive and

542 Timber-frame cross-wing remnant of hall house, now a cottage; Markbeech, Kent; 15C.

543 Flint and brick thatched cottage; Bulford, Wiltshire.

544 Castle-style cottage built for fish keeper; Port Logan, Dumfries and Galloway; c. 1820.

probably lasted no more than a couple of generations. With the advent of enclosure although landlords had an incentive to build farmhouses* there was none to build labourers' housing and they feared that the presence of cottages might increase the poor rate they would have to pay. A description of cottages in Northumberland as late as the 18C is thought to be a fair appraisal of a typical cottage: 'Deplorable, composed of upright timbers fixed in the ground, the interstices wattled and plastered with mud; the roof some thatched and others covered with turf. One little piece of glass to admit the beams of day, and a hearthstone on the ground for a peat and turf fire'. Enlightened 18C landowners led improvements in cottage building. This philanthropy worked in tandem with the creation of the 18C ideal of the remote country house* within landscaped parkland, a type made fashionable by Capability Brown and Humphry Repton. This was done by demolishing unsightly clusters of hovels and replacing them with consciously picturesque cottages. Repton wrote: 'It will frequently happen in a summer's evening that the smoke from this cottage will spread in a thin veil

545 *Cottage orné*, built by Thomas Acland for an employee; Selworthy, Somerset; 1828.

546 Traditional single-storey cottage; Bamburgh, Northumberland; 19C.

547 Stone cottage; Langdale, Cumbria; 1904.

548 Cottage constructed for under £150 built for the Cheap Cottage Exhibition; Letchworth Garden City, Hertfordshire; 1905.

along the glen, ... it must look like what it is, the habitation of a labourer who has the care of the adjoining woods but its simplicity should be the effect of Art and not of accident...'. Such buildings were often termed *cottages ornés* and boasted fancy thatching, bargeboards, patterned chimneys, gables, elaborately glazed windows and loggias with seats. At the turn of the 19C, the idea of a cottage was appropriated by the middle classes, and by the mid-century concerns at the loss of many neglected agricultural cottages resulted in the setting of competitions to find affordable new models for landowners. The word cottage lost its purely rural connotations at the end of the Victorian period, also being used for cottage estates built by the London County Council in the early 20C. From the early part of the century the cottage was increas-ingly appropriated by town-dwellers as a retreat. Batsford and Fry made a plea for sensitive restoration in *The English Cottage* (1938), where a lady magazine editor describes a Tudor cottage in Sussex as 'just a beautiful shell to be gutted'. They comment that 'her remark set us thinking of the Sunday afternoons of actresses and popular novelists beneath the striped umbrellas: tea, talk and cocktails, with a glimpse of tortured half-timber through the rambler roses'. 7, 13, 37, 61, 63, 66, 69, 71, 76, 86, 92, 93, 120, 121, 147, 155, 160, 164, 165, 181, 193, 195, 241, 242, 276, 280, 281, 283, 335, 346, 349, 362, 372, 385, 387, 388, 394, 405, 406, 412, 424, 425, 430, 433, 434, 436, 458, 490, 494, 500, 542, 543, 544, 545, 546, 547, 548

Country house

Landowners of substance generally built houses of a size and grandeur commensurate with their estates. These country 'seats' derive from the use of the word to 'seat' or settle in a locality, although many of these families might also have had a corresponding town house from which to conduct life during the social season and at Court. In building such country houses their owners were generally keen to display their knowledge of the latest architectural taste chosen from books of engravings. Large country houses continued to be built up to the Edwardian period. The system came to a halt with the outbreak of the First World War after which such houses frequently became an economic problem for their owners. As Noel Coward sang in his 1938 song *The Stately Homes of England*: 'The fact that they have to be rebuilt/ And frequently mortgaged to the hilt/ Is inclined to take the gilt off the gingerbread/ and certainly damps the fun/ Of the eldest son...'. This was the decade when the National Trust set up its Country House scheme. 36, 549, 550, 551

Croft

Any kind of house that is held on a particular type of tenancy. The croft refers to the land rented by the crofter, usually about five hectares with a share in hill grazing. Crofts

549 Hylands, stucco Neo-classical country house; Chelmsford, Essex; 1770s.

550 Waddesdon Manor, French Renaissance-style country house, built for Rothschild family; Aylesbury, Buckinghamshire; 1877–83.

551 Port Lympne, Kent, country house built for Philip Sassoon; Lympne, Kent; 1911–13.

552 Whitewashed rubblestone walls with thatch; North Uist, Highlands.

only appear in the Scottish Highlands and Islands. Traditionally croft houses are associated with a type of single-storey dwelling. As crofting areas are remote, there was no option but to build from material immediately available: stone and thatch, heather or barley straw. 62, 552

Deanery

The Dean is responsible for the fabric and running of the Cathedral building alone, hence, their houses are deaneries. Powerful figures in the medieval church deans' houses reflected this, for example the Old

Deanery Salisbury (1258–74) and Wells Deanery (c.1472–98).

Dower house

A house that is in the possession of a widow for her lifetime, since the dower is a proportion of a deceased husband's estate. The dower house was used when the inheritor moved into the principal house with his family.

Farmhouse

The yeoman farmer rose in number and wealth during the 16C and 17C with a corresponding growth in the building of substantial farmhouses in local stone, timber or brick. Date-stones and initials, usually on lintels or walls, commemorate building dates, marriages and additions. By the end of the 18C smaller farms were no longer viable. New agricultural methods required capital and larger landholdings, giving rise to the gentleman farmer, whose requirements were comfort and a 'polite' house. In the early 19C William Cobbett commented on farmhouses in *Rural Rides*: 'Those that are now erected are mere painted shells, with a mistress within, who is stuck in the place she calls a *parlour* ...the house too neat for a dirty-shoed carter to be allowed to

553 Brick front, on Tudor timber-framed house; Halstead, Essex; late 18C/early 19C (façade).

554 Stone farmhouse; Glen Isla, Perth and Kinross; mid-19C.

555 Waterlow Court, block built for women; Hampstead Garden Suburb, London; 1908–9.

556 Millbank Estate, London County Council high-density flats; Westminster, London; 1900.

557 Entrance to mansion block; Marylebone, London; 1896.

558 Block of riverside flats; Westminster, London; 1970s.

559 Modern Movement block, Highpoint; Highgate, London; 1933–38.

come into...'. Pattern books were published aimed at such farmers: the first probably being Daniel Garret's *Designs, and estimates, of farmhouses, &c.* (1747) which included prices for building in brick or stone. The successful economics of more scientific farming methods were reflected in model farmyards and elegant farmhouses. A manor house* is also a farmhouse in the sense that lords of the manors were also farmers. 29, 65, 239, 243, 249, 524, 553, 554

Flats

Since the Middle Ages Edinburgh's constricted geography made flats in houses of eight or nine storeys common long before the English equivalent emerged. The Scottish term for a floor or storey is a 'flat', and housing was commonly divided horizontally with the wealthiest living at the top, farthest from the stink of the street, but linked by a common stair. Even when the building of the New Town began in the 18C a proportion of houses in a terrace or square would often be divided into flats for middle-class occupation. With the population of cities growing flats provided much needed high-density housing. Block dwellings* built to improve the housing of the working classes were in effect flats. However it was not until the 1880s that the middle classes found an acceptable form — the 'mansion' flat. One of the earliest group was Norman Shaw's Albert Hall Mansions (1880–7) with six storeys, bathrooms, lifts and wine cellars. Some early mansion blocks operated like hotels. J. J. Stevenson in *House Architecture* (1880) explained: 'The system to which the name of "mansions" has been given...are really hotels, in which rooms are taken, not for a night or two, but for periods of years, and are furnished by the occupiers'. Their advantages, he explained, included the convenience of being able to come and go at will, of being freed from the cares of servants and housekeeping, the existence of communal public rooms in which to entertain and a central kitchen from which food could be ordered. The lack of an individual front door

555   558
556
557
559

560   561

562

caused a problem for making calls, but this could be solved by the presence of a porter or 'independent communication by means of a speaking-tube'. Mansion block exteriors were characterised by their lavish decoration, rubbed and moulded brickwork, decorative stonework, ironwork, elaborately glazed windows and grand entrances surmounted by prominent name plaques. Most blocks had a narrow balcony along the façade, usually with cast-iron balustrading. The superior floors remained those on the first and second, the inferior flats being nearer the attic. By the 1930s small blocks of flats were built in suburban areas as well as central city locations with detailing that often proclaimed a fashionably 'moderne' look. The name 'Mansions' was dropped in favour of 'Court', reflecting the fact that many flats were built to enclose a private space. This pared-down style reinforced an essentially modern way of living — small, compact, sometimes servantless — reflected in the existence of central heating, communal restaurants and laundries. Dolphin Square in Westminster even had shops at ground level. Flats such as these were particularly suitable for the increased number of single

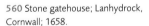

560 Stone gatehouse; Lanhydrock, Cornwall; 1658.

561 Stone arch gatehouse; Charborough, Dorset; c. 1790.

562 Circular stone cottage for lengthsman, Thames and Severn Canal, Chalford, Gloucestershire; early 19C.

working women living independently after the First World War. 185, 207, 208, 210, 211, 212, 213, 216, 238, 259, 308, 312, 316, 317, 319, 356, 408, 411, 417, 420, 431, 475, 486, 555, 556, 557, 558, 559

Gatehouse

The gatehouse comes from castle* architecture: a fortified entrance monitoring those entering the protected space and presenting a forbidding front to the average revolting peasant or disaffected soldier: in the 14C abbeys, cathedral closes, bishop's palaces, monasteries, colleges as well as nobles' houses frequently had gatehouses and at Cleve Abbey it doubled up as lodgings for visitors. An impressive gatehouse combined security with an projection of grandeur. Variations on Classical triumphal arches became popular, providing the perfect gate entrance and space to lodge the gatekeeper and his family. By the 18C it was more usual to build small lodges at entrances. 30, 231, 464, 560, 561

Grange

Originally a grange referred to a granary for a monastic establishment where the abbot or prior was also responsible for the land. Subsequently the term was used for the farmhouse* attached to the tithe barns and granaries. As a house name it was popular for Victorian Gothic Revival or Elizabethan Revival houses.

Hall house

Term given to a house with medieval origins that originally consisted of an open hall (i.e. the total height of the house) where the smoke from the centrally placed fire rose to the roof. Inevitable subsequent improvements mean that it is not possible to recognise this pattern of house from the exterior, although it might have a pronounced central chimney. 386

Lock cottage/ Canal cottage

Canal companies supplied cottages for toll clerks, lock-keepers, bridge-men and lengthsmen (employees who were responsible for the upkeep of a specific length of waterway). Most date from the boom canal-building years of 1790s–1830s. Characteristic details include date labels, weather-vanes and lantern brackets. Some companies had a uniform style: the Shropshire Union used a pattern of yellow brick with a polygonal bay in front, designed by Thomas Telford, already used for his toll houses* on the Holyhead Road.

The Staffordshire and Worcester used an octagonal pattern; Gloucester & Berkeley cottages* had a classical portico, and the Thames & Severn a circular stone shape. 562

Lodge

A lodge can refer to any incidental small house or cottage, although it is usually used to mean a gatekeeper's lodge. It also implies housing for an estate worker, such as a gamekeeper or gardener. Lodges became essential during the 18C when country houses* were set in large parks where entry therefore needed to be monitored far away from the main house. In the 19C it was more common for lodges to match the main house in style rather than be an 'ornament' in the landscape. The lodge became a popular adjunct to the Victorian house of any substance. As late as 1911 R.A.Briggs wrote in *The Essentials of a Country House* that the lodge should be more expensive than the ordinary cottage* since it should 'foreshadow, in a quiet way, the House'. The term lodge is also used, particularly in Scotland, for houses built for sporting activities in remote places. 82, 91, 108, 152, 157, 193, 196, 404, 522, 563, 564, 565

Longhouse

Ancient building type that combined living areas for humans and animals under the same roof and usually separated by a through passage. Common in the medieval period it survived on upland areas until the 17C/18C. 239

Maisonette

The term occasionally appeared in the 19C meaning 'little house' but was used in the early 20C to describe a purpose-built single house divided horizontally to produce cheaper accommodation. On the exterior this arrangement is

563 Rotunda lodge with colonnade; Dodington Park, Gloucestershire; late 18C.

564 Scottish baronial-style lodge to Cally House; Gatehouse of Fleet, Dumfries and Galloway; 1870s.

565 Jacobean Revival lodge with sundial on gable; Belton House, Lincolnshire; 1830s.

563
564
565
566
567
568
569 570

only apparent by paired front doors set within one porch. Later use of the word often suggested space over two floors resulting from the splitting of a large house. Small, four-storey blocks during the 1950s and 1960s were also split internally.

Manor house

The manor — church and king excepted — was the main unit of administration in the feudal system, therefore the manor house with its hall was the focal meeting point and courtroom for the community (although as few as one in eight or ten manors probably had resident lords). Manor houses are therefore among the oldest houses extant, and were the only substantial building within the area apart from the church. Some early manors were probably fortified with moats and battlements. 75, 112, 159, 178, 275, 395, 566

Manse

In medieval times a manse referred to a measure of land regarded as sufficient for a whole family. It now refers to a house lived in by a minister in any Scottish parish.

Mews

Urban stables built along an alley or yard with accommodation for grooms above. The term originates from the Royal Stables at Charing Cross, which were built on the site where the royal hawks were mewed (perched to moult). As carriages, horses and grooms did not fit into the terrace housing* of 18C squares and streets it was necessary to accommodate them in mews, which for the most part ran behind the terrace along the back of the gardens. Housing shortages after the Second World War and the fact that mews were generally in expensive areas of the city meant that most were converted into fashionably compact houses, as Michael Flanders and Donald Swann sang in their 1956 song *Design for Living*: 'We live in a most amusing mews — ever so very Contemporary'. 432, 567

Model housing

Prince Albert's model cottage*, exhibited in the 1851 Great Exhibition, was an early use of the term. By the beginning of the 20C reformers and philanthropists attempted to address the shortage of decent accommodation with a range of different housing types

566 Owlpen Manor; Uley, Gloucestershire; 15C/17C.

567 Mews with pillared entrance; South Kensington, London; c. 1870.

568 Prince Consort's Model Cottages; Windsor, Berkshire; c. 1850–60.

569 Model terrace housing built for mill-workers; Saltaire, Yorkshire; 1854–70s.

570 Model housing for Society for Improving the Condition of Labouring Classes; Bloomsbury, London; 1849.

(even whole villages) which were then frequently described as 'model'. These were funded by a multitude of societies, (e.g. Metropolitan Association for Improving the Dwellings of the Industrial Classes), individuals, charitable trusts (e.g. Peabody, Guinness), employers (railways companies, mill-owners) and city corporations. Many schemes were published with plans, in the manner of the earlier pattern books. The 1890 Housing of Working Classes Act made local authorities responsible and gave them the power to compulsorily purchase land for housing. 41, 67, 206, 568, 569, 570

Pele tower

Housing dating from the Border Wars between Scotland and England which ran intermittently from the 15C to 17C. The 'pele' is the name for the enclosure into which the cattle were herded in times of danger. People lived in tower houses built within the pele: three or four floors high, stone-built with fortifying features such as battlements, loopholes and turrets. 571

Prefabs

A year after the government had established its Temporary Housing Programme in 1944 the first inhabitants moved in during the summer of 1945. Four basic types of pre-fabricated bungalows* were devised, designed to last for ten to fifteen years. The Arcon was a steel frame clad with corrugated asbestos cement sheet, the doors and windows stove enamelled; the Uni-Seco had a timber-frame clad with flat asbestos cement sheet, while the Tarran was timber-framed with concrete panels. This was the heaviest to transport but featured in a BBC Home Service programme entitled *Building a Cottage in One Hour*. The most expensive and experimental was the Aluminium bungalow, the prototype of which was exhibited behind Selfridges department store by the Aluminium Development Association in the summer of 1945. In over 150,000 prefabs were erected. 573, 575

Presbytery

Part of a church reserved for the clergy alone and by extension used in medieval times to describe the priest's house. Now only refers to a house lived in by a Roman Catholic priest.

Semi-detached

From the early 18C, double cottages* were common on farms and estates as an economic measure. In the early 19C the semi-detached house used the same principle but became popular

571 Pele tower; near Lowther, Cumbria.

572 Regency stone double villa; Inverleith, Edinburgh; 1820s.

573 Arcon-type prefab; Chelmsford, Essex; late 1940s.

574 Suburban semi-detached house; Palmer's Green, London; 1920s.

575 Tarran-type prefab; Henleaze, Bristol; late 1940s.

571 572

573 574

575

577
576

578

as a way of presenting ostensibly large and spacious houses as part of an attractive villa development, which in fact offered smaller, cheaper houses. The term came into common use in the mid-19C. For subsequent generations of new house buyers after the First World War the semi-detached was a useful solution: since they used up less land than detached houses they were priced more cheaply but at the same time offered more space and privacy than the city terraces*, from which many were hoping to escape. The form also allowed for garages to be built on the non-attached side of the house — an increasingly important feature. 48, 78, 111, 258, 309, 572, 574

Studio

In the Victorian period successful artists began building eclectically styled houses in hitherto unfashionable areas of London, such as Maida Vale and St. John's Wood, which incorporated double-height studio rooms large enough to fill with the props required by genre and history painters. From the mid-19C speculative builders provided more mundane premises for rental

by less successful artists. Conveniently these could often be fitted into odd parcels of land (for example beside railways) which were unsuitable for more conventional housing. The word 'studio' continued to be used throughout the 20C although increasingly it was used to convey an interestingly bohemian (and cramped) living space. The term survives to describe one-room living (e.g. studio flat). 166, 472, 576

Tenement

Literally, this refers to a dwelling that is rented or 'held' and not owned. The term was used principally in Scotland since in Scottish law most houses were 'subinfeudated' or sublet from the monarch down to a baron and so on down the social scale. Tenements continued the tradition established at an early date in Scottish cities whereby the housing was on one 'flat' (or floor) with the common staircase almost an extension of the street. Tenements were built for all classes in Scottish cities, particularly Glasgow, with cheap versions crammed into small plots that were previously gardens. With the overcrowding from the

influx of 19C immigrants from the Highlands these rapidly deteriorated into slum housing and bought the word into disrepute. By the end of the century work was being done by organisations such as the City Improvement Trust (in Glasgow) to build tenements of a good standard. 577, 578

Terrace

The first terrace to be called as such was the 18C Adelphi built by the Adam Brothers (the word presumably refers to the garden terrace providing a promenade fronting the Thames), although in a

576 Studio house; Chelsea, London; c. 1880.

577 Abbey Strand tenements; Edinburgh; late 15C/early 16C.

578 Stone tenements; West End, Glasgow; late 19C.

579 Royal Crescent (the first terrace in crescent form); Bath; 1764–67.

580 French Second Empire style terrace; Kensington, London; 1883.

581 Sandstone terrace; Ayr, Ayrshire; late 19C.

582 Terrace in Italianate style; Cheltenham, Gloucestershire; 1840s.

583 Stone terrace housing opening onto street; Elland, Yorkshire; mid-19C.

584 Brick-and-glass terrace; Southwark, London; late 1980s.

585 One-up, one-down stone end-of-terrace house; Marsden, Yorkshire; mid-19C.

sense the joined row of individual houses of Vicar's Close in Wells (1348) is the first terrace housing in Britain. The terrace treats a row of individual houses as a single unit, omitting variation in favour of conformity. As a result the accommodation is vertical with a few rooms at each level, in some cases neatly separating the family from its servants. Terraces were built in thousands of 18C and 19C developments all over Britain, and many were speculations by builders with very flimsy specifications. Terraces could also be bent into crescents (and occasionally circuses), following the line of the landscape and giving picturesque views of hills and sea as at Bath, Buxton and Brighton. Terraces followed current architectural style, so the smooth façades of the 18C Georgian terraces progressed in the 19C to a heavier style with rustication, balustrading and a portico porch. Stucco was used extensively, in many cases conveniently disguising cheap building materials. Towards the end of the 19C there was a tendency to build terraces that might appear as a sequence of semi-detached* houses, or even cottages* with bays, 'Gothic' gables and elaborate porches which created a zigzag roofline. The terrace is probably the most archetypal British housing type, providing the much-loved individual front entrance and patch of back garden. 10, 26, 28, 40, 43, 47, 49, 56, 60, 67, 84, 94, 101, 107, 118, 119, 122, 123, 124, 125, 127, 128, 143, 144, 145, 146, 148, 168, 173, 174, 198, 232, 234, 270, 284, 288, 300, 307, 315, 318, 319, 333, 337, 344, 358, 361, 363, 383, 384, 389, 391, 392, 393, 409, 423, 448, 454, 455, 456, 457, 459, 461, 466, 473, 474, 484, 489, 498, 501, 513, 579, 580, 581, 582, 583, 584, 585

Toll house

Cottage* for toll gatekeeper on a turnpike road (in which a toll was paid to travel a length of road thus enabling the money to be spent on its upkeep). This housing was provided free by the turnpike trust who employed both men and women to assess and collect correct dues. Tolls were unpopular with the local population and led to minor riots. Toll houses abutted the road and were built with multiple windows facing out along the highway to get a clear view of oncoming traffic. To achieve this they were usually circular or polygonal and many had castellations and Gothick elements, popular at the time. Turnpikes disappeared after the expansion of the railways in the 1840s. 586, 587, 588

Tower block

New building techniques involving steel frames, reinforced concrete, pre-fabricated systems and improved lift technology made multi-storey high-density blocks a solution to mid-20C housing problems. The provision of daylight was another factor that dominated post-Second World War design and the steel-frame building (box frame and cross walls) allowed not only for height (and high living density) but also for almost continuous windows around the exterior. Alongside these considerations was the belief that attractive open spaces could be created at ground level, as, with frame construction, the walls could be omitted and the building could be supported on pilotis or piers. The first flats* over 20 storeys high were built by the London County Council in Warwick Crescent, begun in 1961. Councils such as Edinburgh, Glasgow, Southampton, Liverpool and Newcastle followed suit. 215, 365, 589, 590, 591

586 Circular castellated toll house; Wootton-under-Edge, Gloucestershire; early 19C.

587 Polygonal thatched toll house with Gothick windows; Chew Magna, Somerset; early 19C.

588 Gabled toll house with bargeboards; Bruton, Somerset; early 19C.

Tower house

House for lairds in Scotland (anyone could style himself as a laird, provided that he had land). Originally built as a defensible house, the tower house became the favourite form for houses built in the countryside, even when the need for fortification was long past.

Vicarage
(also rectory, parsonage)

Vicar's closes, for example attached to Wells and Chichester cathedrals, were the quarters first established for vicars. It was not until after the Reformation that vicars could marry, and equally the religious upheavals of the 16 and 17C were not conducive to establishing vicarages. However by the 18C the church was one of few alternative careers for younger sons of the gentry who therefore required substantial houses. P. F. Robinson wrote in *Village Architecture* (1830) on parsonages, that they 'should be erected in the Old English character;... although some little decoration may be employed to increase its interest and general character (it should be) modest and unassuming, ...the open porch indicating a welcome to the poor as well as the rich'. After the Pluralities Act of 1838 vicars were encouraged to live in the immediate vicinity of their churches and many new churches appeared in fast-growing towns. This resulted in a spate of vicarage-building, often in the Gothic Revival style (the style of Christianity) which sent a clear signal of change from the lax days of the previous century. In the 20C large vicarages became an increasing burden and any new buildings were distinctly modest.
518, 592, 593

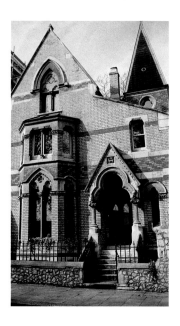

589 Point block/cluster block, Keeling House; Bethnal Green, London; 1960.

590 Point blocks; Leith, Edinburgh; 1970s.

591 Slab block; Lower Kingsdown, Bristol; 1960s.

592 Former rectory; Burnham Market, Norfolk; early 19C.

593 Gothic Revival vicarage; Camden, London; c. 1861.

Villa

A description deriving from Classical Rome, the villa was a country retreat from town life, perhaps to farming or retirement. The idea was revived in the Italian Renaissance, for example in the villas by Palladio outside Venice. Lord Burlington built his villa at Chiswick, a few miles from his town house in Piccadilly, and decorated it with scrupulously Classical ornament. The term returned to general use in the late 18C/early 19C to describe stylish middle-class houses set on the outskirts of town within their own ornamental garden. During the 19C the term descended the social scale and began to smack of suburban pretension. Plaques such as 'Rose Villa' soon appeared above terrace* house doors and 'villadom' suggested a narrow-minded outlook. 11, 12, 16, 85, 48, 78, 258, 594, 595, 596, 597

Wealden house

Timber-framed house with central hall and jettied side wings, characteristic of the Kent and Sussex Weald (although they do occur elsewhere). The roof spans the whole building creating a deep eave in the central section. The form persisted until the 1530s. 3

Weaver's house

House or cottage dating from the pre-industrial revolutionary period (and therefore pre-factory) when weavers produced piece-work at home. They are characterised by long ranges of windows along the upper storeys to let in as much light as possible. They only occur in cotton and wool areas such as Yorkshire and Lancashire, although similar window arrangements appear in Hugenot silkweavers' houses in Spitalfields, London. 240

594 South front of Chiswick House, Palladian villa built by Lord Burlington; Chiswick, London; 1725–59.

595 Gothick-style Regency villa; Seaton, Devon; early 19C.

596 'Swift Villa'; Dalkeith, Midlothian; c. 1900.

597 'Raglan Villa'; Bath; c. 1870.

Index of Counties and Unitary Authorities

England

Bath 28, 125, 128, 152, 202, 203, 232, 233, 234, 341, 343, 419, 519, 579

Bedfordshire 106, 195

Berkshire 13, 426, 448, 450, 568

Bristol 77, 81, 124, 142, 146, 191, 230, 324, 451, 514, 575, 591

Buckinghamshire 42, 83, 177, 404, 500, 550

Cambridgeshire 33, 173

Cheshire 41, 90, 103, 168, 292, 307, 409, 461

Cornwall 75, 178, 428, 560,

Cumbria 105, 37, 147, 253, 547, 571

Derbyshire 54, 66, 67, 137, 179, 394

Devon 11, 538, 595

Dorset 7, 8, 561

Durham 40

Essex 20, 22, 27, 29, 73, 44, 50, 63, 79, 80, 82, 88, 100, 129, 138, 140, 181, 229, 263, 270, 273, 279, 309, 311, 339, 350, 355, 364, 368, 371, 372, 386, 396, 397, 399, 402, 410, 430, 431, 433, 463, 464, 483, 511, 516, 527, 536, 549, 553, 573

Gloucestershire 15, 21, 36, 46, 53, 57, 64, 92, 95, 99, 119, 163, 160, 175, 176, 189, 194, 227, 228, 245, 272, 286, 320, 385, 477, 495, 530, 562, 563, 566, 582, 586

Hampshire 47, 58, 61, 117, 156, 435, 493

Herefordshire 535

Hertfordshire 49, 70, 212, 291, 338, 358, 389, 453, 548

Isle of Wight 534

Kent 65, 183, 370, 374, 405, 425, 452, 496, 542, 551

Lancashire 34, 281, 287

Lincolnshire 76, 565

London 4, 12, 18, 19, 24, 26, 30, 31, 43, 52, 55, 56, 60, 74, 78, 91, 93, 109, 110, 111, 115, 122, 123, 127, 136, 139, 143, 144, 145, 148, 154, 158, 162, 166, 167, 170, 172, 174, 185, 186, 187, 201, 206, 207, 208, 210, 211, 212, 214, 215, 216, 238, 258, 259, 262, 264, 265, 267, 271, 285, 288, 294, 296, 298, 298, 299, 304, 305, 306, 308, 310, 312, 313, 314, 315, 316, 317, 319, 321, 323, 325, 327, 328, 333, 334, 336, 337, 340, 344, 349, 351, 353, 354, 356, 357, 361, 363, 365, 373, 375, 376, 377, 378, 379, 380, 381, 382, 383, 384, 392, 393, 407, 408, 411, 414, 415, 416, 417, 420, 422, 427, 432, 439, 441, 443, 447, 448, 455, 459, 462, 466, 468, 469, 470, 471, 472, 475, 476, 481, 484, 485, 486, 487, 502, 504, 506, 512, 513, 528, 531, 539, 555, 556, 557, 558, 559, 567, 570, 574, 576, 580, 584, 589, 593,

594

Merseyside 456

Middlesex 139, 357

Norfolk 9, 68, 196, 224, 250, 283, 289, 346, 442, 515, 541, 592

Northamptonshire 98, 247

Northumberland 165, 546

Nottinghamshire 6

Oxfordshire 1, 86, 171, 274, 276, 277, 280, 282, 284, 301, 444, 480, 503, 507, 518

Rutland 141, 532

Shropshire 153, 403, 406, 521

Somerset 2, 14, 23, 32, 39, 51, 59, 69, 94, 104, 112, 116, 130, 131, 135, 188, 193, 225, 236, 242, 266, 318, 436, 454, 474, 478, 479, 482, 490, 497, 510, 523, 526, 545, 587, 588, 597

Staffordshire 537

Suffolk 87, 133, 149, 220, 248, 290, 300, 345, 367, 369, 390, 398, 400, 401, 438, 445, 446, 457, 458, 489, 520

Surrey 5, 134, 192, 218, 322, 330, 362, 413, 412, 434, 440, 468, 505, 529

Sussex 3, 16, 107, 118, 182, 190, 200, 205, 226, 332, 423, 424, 473, 499, 540

Tyne and Wear 217

Warwickshire 120, 347

Wiltshire 159, 161, 231, 246, 251, 275, 326, 329, 331, 342, 492, 509, 543

Worcestershire 395

Yorkshire 72, 95, 102, 108, 113, 114, 151, 155, 240, 243, 249, 268, 278, 467, 525, 569, 583, 585

Scotland

Aberdeenshire 241

Argyll and Bute 38, 360

Ayrshire 164, 388, 522, 581

Dumfries and Galloway 97, 221, 223, 303, 391, 533, 544, 564

Edinburgh 84, 101, 208, 222, 295, 302, 488, 498, 572, 577, 590

Fife 71, 269

Glasgow 578

Highlands 491, 552

Midlothian 596

Perth and Kinross 244, 348, 554

Scottish Borders 45

Western Isles 62

Wales

Cardiff 48, 126, 132, 184, 209, 237, 418, 501

Gwynedd 17, 239, 494

Pembrokeshire 25, 387, 508

Index of Architects

Adam, Robert and Bros. 197, 295, 376, 377, 378, 481

Adam, Robert 156

Aldington and Craig 42, 177

Baillie Scott, M.H. 555

Baker and May 548

Baker, H. and E. Willmott 461

Barradale, Isaac 532

Bennett and Bidwell 71

Burlington, Lord 594

Burton, Decimus 383

Burton, Richard 265

Chambers, Sir William 7

CZWG 170

Darbishire, H. A. 93, 206

De Syllas, Justin 52

Destailleur, H. 550

Dryden, Edward 270

Dunster, Bill 218

Erskine, Ralph 217

Future Systems 24, 187

Goldfinger, Erno 215

Gwynne, Patrick 503

Halfpenny, William 36, 189

Hill, Oliver 50

Hopkins, Michael and Patty 186

Johnson, John 593

Knott, Ralph 308

Lacey, Nick 558

Lasdun, Sir Denys 589

Leech, John 311

Lescaze, William 359

Leverton, Thomas 327, 380, 478

Lifschutz Davidson 584

Lutyens, Edwin 450

Lyons, Eric 427

Mackmurdo, A.H. 166

Menteith, W. 316

Milne, James 84

Morgan, Guy 312

Nash, John 361

Norman Shaw, Richard 406

Papworth, J.B. 85

Parker and Unwin 337

Paxton, Sir Joseph 66

Petter J and Nissen 497

Pilkington, E.C. 208

Playfair, W.H. 199

Proctor Matthews 26, 43

Roberts, Henry 570

Robinson, Sir Thomas 151

Scrymgeour, W. H. 557

Segal, Walter 214

Smythson, Robert 96, 113, 278

Tait, Thomas 20

Taylor, Reginald Minton 556

Tecton, 211, 214, 559

Terry, Quinlan 72

Toms, R. 210

Voysey, C. F. A. 355

Wigglesworth, Sarah and Jeremy Till 528

Wilds, Amon 107, 190

Wood, John the Elder 232, 234

Wood, John the Younger 579

Wren, Sir Christopher 539

Wyatt Thomas 592

Wyatt, James 563